Dynamic Range

Bill Tennessen's Photographic Journey Through
Late 20th Century Milwaukee

Edited by Charlie Tennessen

Original black and white photos by Bill Tennessen,
now in the collection of the Haggerty Museum

Color photos by Charlie Tennessen

Captions, chapter descriptions, and interview courtesy of
the Haggerty Museum at Marquette University

ISBN: 979-8-9929134-0-8
Library of Congress Control Number: 2025934750

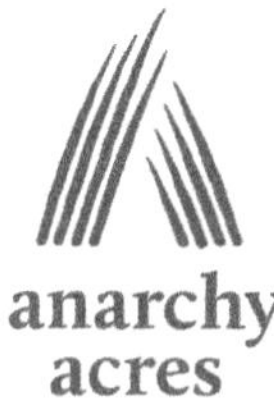

anarchy
acres

Acknowledgements

There are many people who contributed to the Dynamic Range exhibit at the Haggerty Museum and who otherwise inspired this book. The exhibition that this book is based on ran at the Haggerty Museum at Marquette University from January 19 through May 12, 2024. The exhibition was curated by Lynne Shumow (Haggerty Museum Curator for Academic Engagement) in collaboration with Dr. Robert Smith (Marquette University Harry G. John Professor of History and Director of the Center for Urban Research, Teaching and Outreach—CURTO) and Mia Phifer (Education and Research Coordinator at America's Black Holocaust Museum). Additional assistance was provided by Kate Rose, Caroline Bielski, Sebastien Brown, Sophia Furman, Logan Glembin, Niktalia Jules, and Adamali De La Cruz.

Exhibition and brochure design by Daniel Herro (Haggerty Museum Head Designer and Preparator).

Support for the exhibition was generously provided by the Marquette University Women's Council Endowment Fund.

Design consultation by Barb Paulini

Additional thanks include Bob Pecher, Kate Tennessen, Margaret Tennessen and Carol Tennessen.

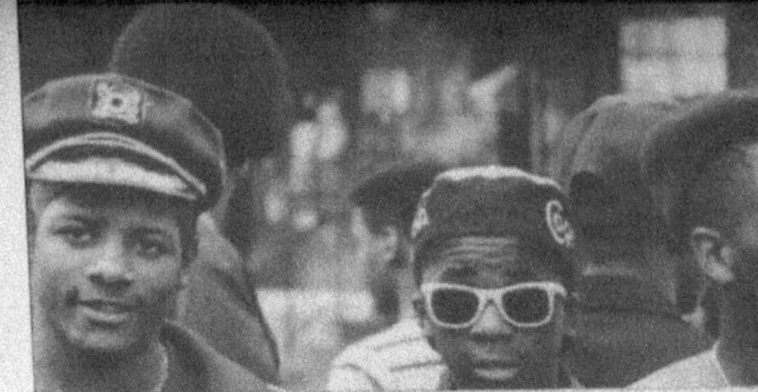
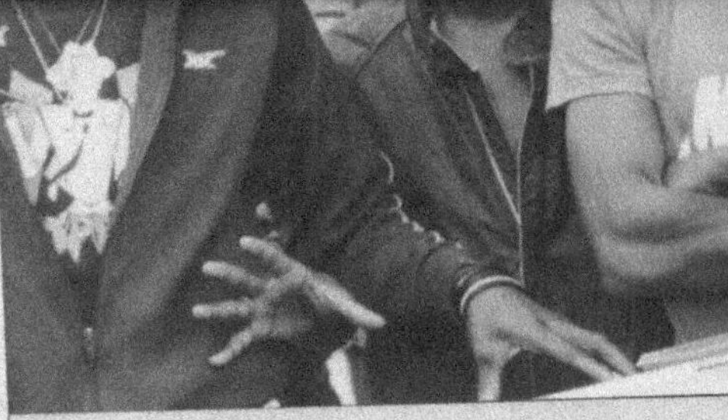
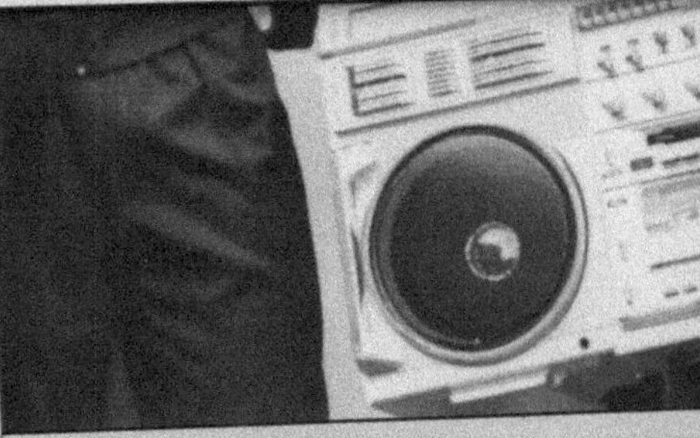

Dynamic Range
Photographs by Bill Tennessen
HOURS
Monday - Saturday
10 a.m. - 4:30 p.m.
Sunday - Closed
Free Admission

Contents

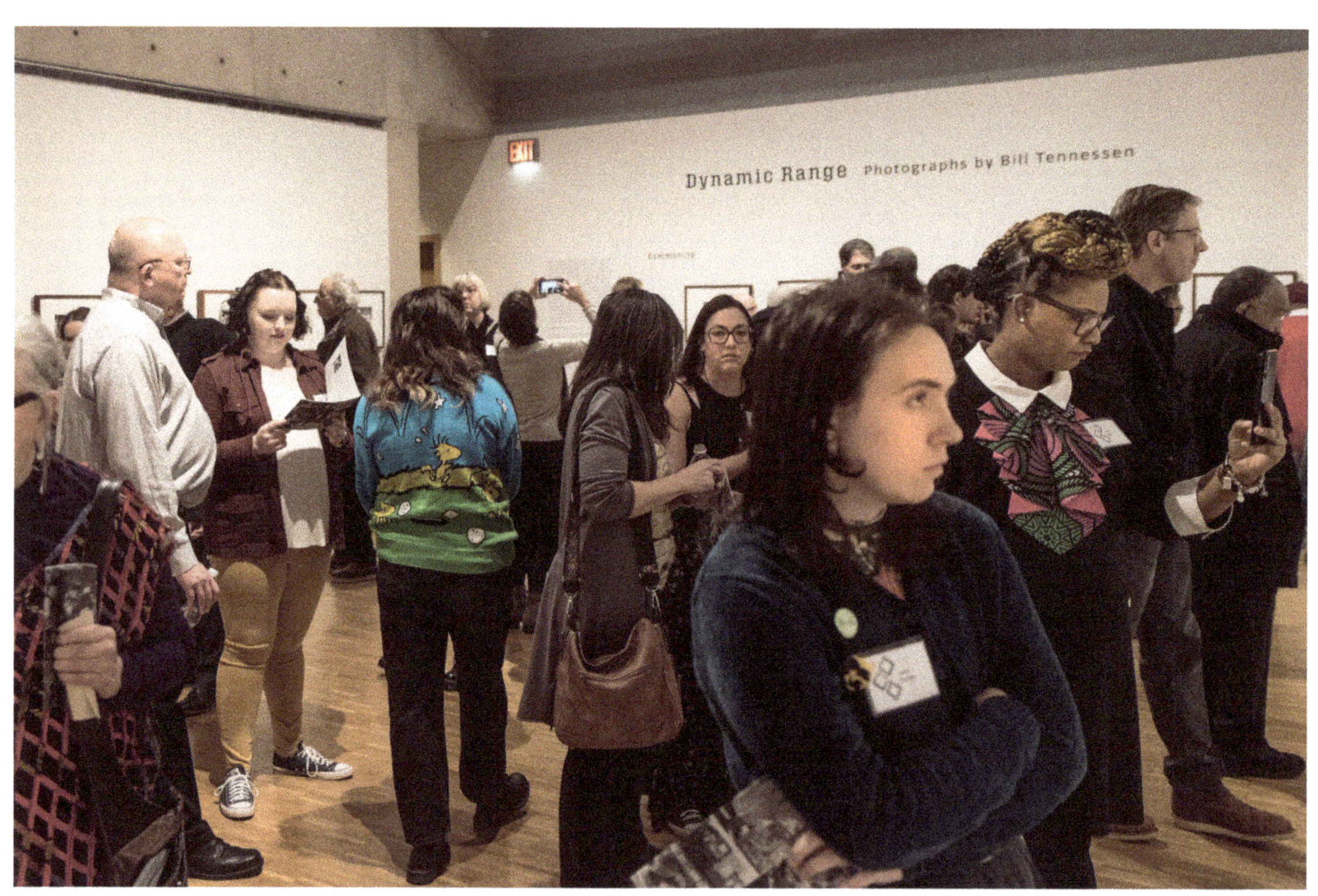

Opening reception, January 18, 2024

Editor's Note

Growing up with my family in the 70s and 80s, it was forbidden to ever decline being photographed. If a camera was pointed at someone, that person was expected to stop what they were doing, look at the camera, and smile. Probably half of the photos taken in the household were tests of some sort—lens test, film test, shutter test, darkroom test, etc. The camera might be anything from a tiny Minox spy camera, a beautiful 5x7 view camera, or a vintage 35mm Leica. Ultimately, Dad took many more photos than the rest of the household combined. If you wanted to find Dad in those years, you looked in the darkroom.

Fast forward to around 2022, I remembered those remarkable photos Dad took of things going on in the City of Milwaukee. At that time, he was photographing for the Milwaukee Community Journal, the Milwaukee Boys & Girls Club, and for his own artistic enjoyment. I started sharing the photos with friends and wondered if there were a gallery or museum that could put on a retrospective show of Dad's work.

In the spring of 2023, I was able to interest the Haggerty Museum of Art at Marquette University to do a show featuring this historic photography. Dad and I began pulling boxes of old photos and negatives out of the basement, looking for "the good stuff." A fantastic team, led by Haggerty curator Lynne Shumow, visited my parent's house at least three times to review and select photos.

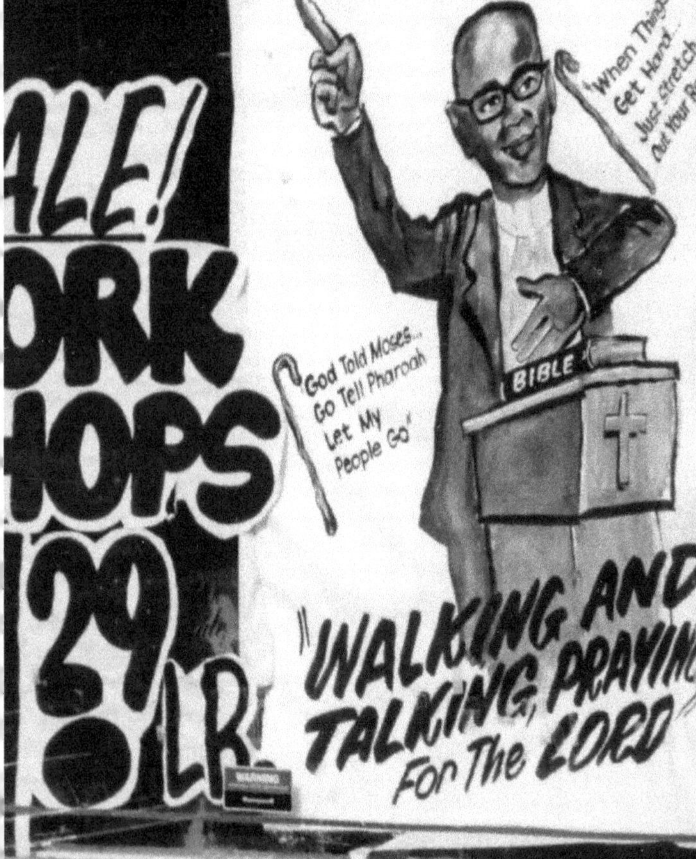
SALE!
TURKEY
NECKS
49¢ lb.
SALE!
PORK
CHOPS
129 lb.
"When Things
Get Hard...
Just Stretch
Out Your Rod!"
God Told Moses...
Go Tell Pharoah
Let My
People Go"
BIBLE
"WALKING AND
TALKING, PRAYING,
For The LORD"

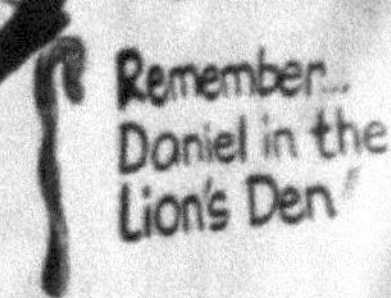

JIFFY MUFFIN
MIX...
4/99¢
"WALKING
AND
TALKING,
PRAYING
FOR THE
LORD"
"Remember...
Little David
& The Giant
Goliath"
BIBLE
Remember...
Daniel in the
Lion's Den"

The Haggerty team initially selected around 100 photos, and over the course of months whittled them down to 50 of the most interesting and beautiful. The amount of research they put into the photographs was astounding. I remember Dad's jaw dropping when he realized they had somehow learned the name of a firefighter he had photographed at a Milwaukee fire, from 40 years ago.

The show ran at the Haggerty Museum from January 19 through May 12, 2024. I believe it was the most popular art show in recent memory at the museum. The opening was very well attended and everyone in my family went back for multiple viewings.

This book is my best attempt to record the show as it appeared at the Haggerty. Forty-six of the photos are scans of Dad's original silver nitrate prints. I've scanned the actual prints that Dad made in the darkroom and attempted to render these prints exactly as they appear when I had them in my hand.

The remaining four photos are digital prints from the original negatives. The photo captions and descriptions are all the hard work of the Haggerty staff. Dad and I have changed a few small details which we believe were in error. The remaining errors, omissions, and faults are my own.

–Charlie Tennessen, Editor

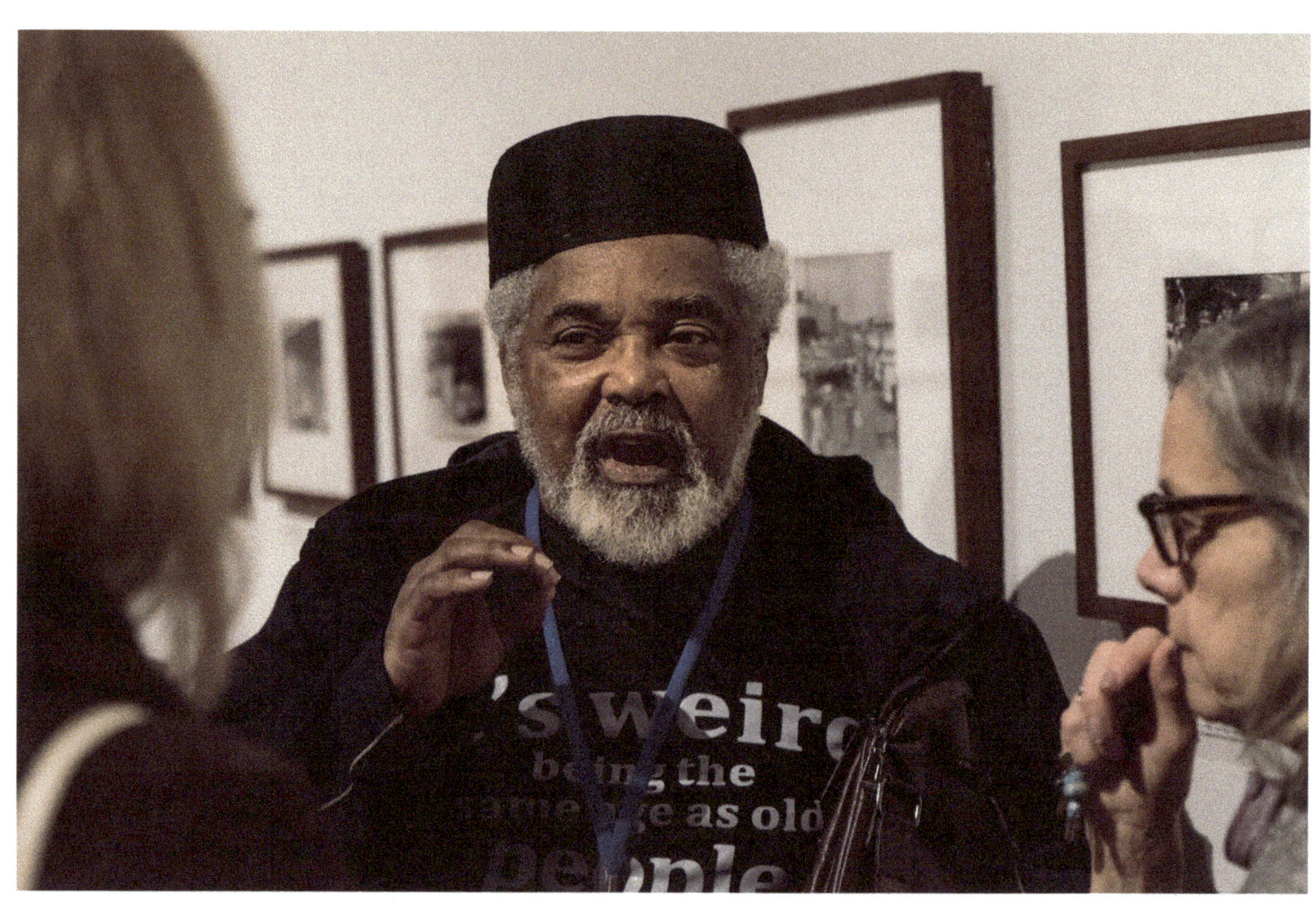

Mikel Holt, Founding Editor and Associate Publisher of the
Milwaukee Community Journal

Forward

An old African adage posits that working alongside a friend makes the time fly and provides a more perfect product. I was thinking of that when I reflected on my decades of service alongside Bill Tennessen. Not only has he become a great friend, but his photographic contributions have also helped make the Milwaukee Community Journal an award-winning publication. Bill's unique and memorable photography helped place the publication in the upper sphere of newspapers. Locally, his photographs sparked interest and grew our readership. Folks sought out the paper to view his interpretive sports photos. His candid communal shots brought both tears and praise.

As a photojournalist myself, I can attest to the quality of his work. His photos are not only distinctive but intuitive. Bill's photos capture moments in history, scenarios that fellow Black Press photographer Pat A. Robinson refers to as a unique "documentation of our lives." Bill captured the essence of Black life. I once described him as a Gordon Parks clone, a historian who shared his photographic eye with our readership.

I attended military photography school after my tour of service in Vietnam. I learned about lighting, composition, and lenses. I won the National Newspaper Publishers Association's (NNPA) 'Best News Photo' Award decades ago because I had acquired 'the eye,' that exceptional quality I learned during lessons taught by local greats like Ken Lumpkin, Harry Kemp, and Bill Tennessen. From them, I learned to not just 'look' but to 'see,' to compose a story within the image, to record history.

Out of the blue, and without a job notice, Bill showed up at the Community Journal offices one day offering his services. Surprisingly, he didn't seek compensation; he required only a press pass and an opportunity. I was initially hesitant, given that Bill didn't carry the latest or most expensive equipment across his chest. Long before the digital era, he nonetheless provided a portfolio that showed me he possessed a unique skill set, which impressed me enough to take him on as a freelance photographer. His first photos of a Milwaukee Bucks game were not only worthy of front-page placement but also a picture frame.

Over the years, we frequently put his photos on the front page of the MCJ, as they became an enticement for readers to pick up the newspaper and admire his additional handiwork. We rarely assigned Bill to cover a social or cultural event, but that didn't stop him from appearing at them to take photos. His photos of former President Jimmy Carter doing carpentry work for Habitat For Humanity, for example, were a pleasant surprise.

And even though we sometimes found ourselves at the same event, I would lay down my camera, assuming his shots were worthy of placement. Such was the case with the photos of Milwaukee's Juneteenth celebration that Bill would take almost every year during his tenure with the newspaper. One time, he climbed up a Milwaukee Fire Department ladder truck to photograph the depth of the massive crowd walking up and down Third Street (now Dr. Martin Luther King, Jr. Drive).

Though he was invited as a guest to my wedding years ago, Bill came equipped with his camera and shot photos of it. A black and white wide-screen photo he took of the event graces my parent's wall to this day.

Bill worked his way into our Milwaukee Community Journal family, coming in as a foster child, then an adopted son, and finally a full-fledged blood brother of the family and was introduced as such at our most recent annual celebration.

I gotta a lot of love for Bill. I appreciate his talent, but more importantly, I love his gentle spirit and quiet humor. He is a brother by another mother and culture. His photography has stood the test of time. In fact, Bill Tennessen's photos are timeless and paint a portrait of Black life that will be included in our chapter of Black History.

    –Mikel Holt, founding editor and associate publisher of the Milwaukee Community Journal

L - SHERIFF RICHARD ARTISON
JIM MOODY
HILLARY CLINTON
BILL CLINTON
R - SEN. HERB KOHL

RAY ALLEN GOING AROUND
ALLEN IVERSON IN GAME 6
OF PLAYOFFS.

BUCKS WIN & TIE SERIES 3-3

10-20-92

KO-THI AT PABST THEATRE
FOR
20 TH ANNIVERSARY CELEBRATION

- 2001 -
BILL TENNESSEN

6 - 17 - 89

2ND LEFT - MOTHER OF ERNEST LACY
FATHER OF ERNEST LACY

FULL HOUSE

AT INNER CITY ARTS FESTIVAL - 7-30-89

- 1989 -
BILL TENNESSEN

CIRCA - 1980's

ARTIST REYNALDO HERNANDEZ

BILL TENNESSEN

JUNETEENTH DAY - 1983

9-17-91

- 1986 -
BILL TENNESSEN

MURAL ON 5TH & NORTH (LENA'S BIG VALUE SUPERMARKET)

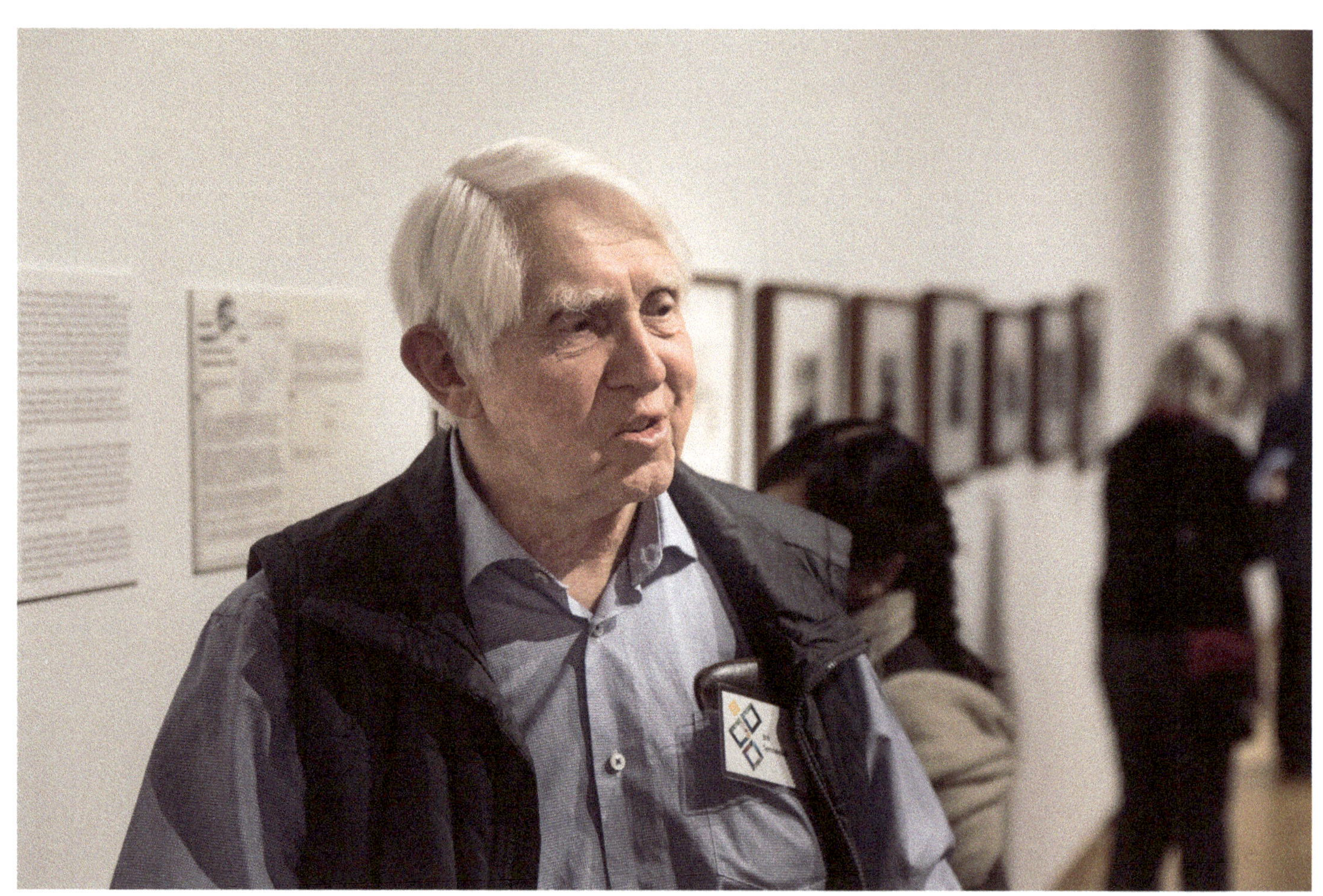

Milwaukee Photographer Bill Tennessen

Interview with Bill Tennessen

The following interview was conducted by Kate Rose, Academic Engagement Fellow for the Haggerty, on October 5, 2023, at the home of Bill Tennessen.

KR: WHEN DID YOU GET YOUR FIRST CAMERA, AND WHAT WERE SOME OF YOUR FIRST FORAYS INTO PHOTOGRAPHY?

BT: My first camera was a Kodak film sized 116 box camera that belonged to my mother. I might still have some original negatives and several rolls of film from that camera. I put a darkroom in the basement of my parents' home when I was about thirteen years old. I was, at the time, rather influenced by fine art photography, although I wouldn't have known any fine art photographers by name. I can remember going to take a picture of a bridge in McGovern Park, which is right off of Silver Spring Drive. I remember thinking that if I just pointed the camera at the right angle at this bridge, I could take a fine art photograph.

KR: SKIPPING AHEAD, YOU ATTENDED MARQUETTE UNIVERSITY. WHY DID YOU CHOOSE MARQUETTE?

BT: There was a choice between UW-Madison and Marquette, but my father's side of the family was Catholic, and he preferred I go to a Catholic university. I remember that it was a financial struggle for my father to send me to Marquette. If I recall correctly, the University of Wisconsin-Madison cost $12 to attend and Marquette cost $165. I'm not sure if that was per semester or per year.

KR: WHAT WAS YOUR MAJOR AT MARQUETTE?

BT: Business Administration. I believe the major was called Real Estate and Insurance at that time.

KR: I UNDERSTAND YOU OWNED YOUR OWN BUSINESS, AND THAT WAS WHAT ALLOWED YOU TO TAKE OFF THE TIME YOU NEEDED TO DO PHOTOGRAPHY. IS THAT CORRECT?

BT: I began working for the Fidelity Appraisal Company in 1960. After about twenty years the owner wanted to step back and offered to sell the business to my business partner, Tom, and me. We paid for the purchase over a ten-year period and continued to operate the company until about fifteen years ago, when we both decided to retire. Due to the nature of the business, it did not require both Tom and me to be there every day from nine to five. This allowed us time for other activities, such as travel and photography.

KR: WAS THE MILWAUKEE COMMUNITY JOURNAL THE FIRST NEWSPAPER OR JOURNAL THAT YOU PHOTOGRAPHED FOR?

BT: I recall going in with some spot news photos to the Milwaukee Journal, and they would buy them for a very nominal price, $10 or $15 or something. I had no formal association with other newspapers prior to my work with the Milwaukee Community Journal.

KR: HOW DID YOU GET CONNECTED WITH THEM?

BT: My connection to the Milwaukee Community Journal began around the time of the [Ernest] Lacy inquest in the early 1980s. I was taking pictures for the Boys & Girls Clubs of Greater Milwaukee and the YWCA. Of course, those groups loved to get publicity, so I would take pictures of their activities and then take those photos to the Milwaukee Community Journal with a little narrative to try to get them published in the paper. After I provided photos of the Lacy inquest and other events, their sports editor, Cal Patterson, asked me to photograph the Milwaukee Bucks basketball games. He was a big fan of the Bucks. That's how I got started photographing basketball. Cal also ran the cooking department. They had quite a cooking department, including an event every other year called "Men Who Cook." I remember photographing the chefs, which was a little more unusual in those days than it might be now. During that time, I also photographed Packer football games, politicians, entertainers, and celebrities who visited Milwaukee, and many other events for the paper.

KR: ARE YOU STILL WORKING FOR THE MILWAUKEE COMMUNITY JOURNAL?

BT: My name is still on the masthead at the Milwaukee Community Journal, and I am very proud of that. Their main photographer for many years was Harry Kemp, who also photographed for the Milwaukee Courier, another central city newspaper. Harry died in 2011, and his sister Yvonne is now the paper's lead photographer, with contributions from other photographers, including me.

KR: EVERYTHING WE HAVE IN THE HAGGERTY'S SHOW WAS SHOT ON FILM AND DEVELOPED BY YOU, BUT NOW WHEN YOU WORK IT'S MOSTLY DIGITAL, CORRECT?

BT: Yes, that's why you won't find any hard prints after a certain date. I can't tell you the exact date, but it's going to be in the 2000s when I started shooting with digital cameras.

KR: WOULD YOU BE ABLE TO TALK A BIT ABOUT YOUR DARKROOM PROCESS?

BT: I'm still set up with the darkroom, but I have not made any prints in about five years. It's a storeroom right now, but I could set it up again in half a day—all the plumbing is still there, the sinks and enlargers and so on. The process of developing film is what makes a photographer produce a photograph; it's just as important as picking the subject or aiming the camera. That said, I wouldn't give up digital for anything right now. It's so simple for me. I have my computer set up with various automatic light balancing tools, and I can put the digital file in, and in a matter of five minutes I can produce a reasonably good copy that will look good in the paper. In the darkroom, I might work for half an hour to get one print just the way I want it.

KR: SO, WOULD YOU SAY THAT SOME OF THE JOY IN PHOTOGRAPHY FOR YOU IS THE SKILL IT TAKES ON THE DEVELOPING END?

BT: I've always thought so. Yes, I have a lot more understanding and respect for a photographer that does the whole thing, from clicking the shutter to producing the finished print.

KR: THERE IS A PHOTOGRAPH THAT WAS AN IMMEDIATE FAVORITE WHEN WE WERE LOOKING THROUGH YOUR WORK, DATED 1985, OF A GROUP OF INDIVIDUALS GATHERED AROUND A BOOM BOX. DO YOU HAVE ANY RECOLLECTION OF THAT MOMENT, WHO THOSE PEOPLE WERE, OR WHAT WAS GOING ON?

BT: Oh, yes. I remember. I did not pose that photograph or round them up. They posed for me and asked me to take their picture. It was at a Juneteenth Day celebration. I took two pictures, and that one turned out.

KR: SPEAKING OF THE JUNETEENTH DAY CELEBRATIONS, YOU'RE A WHITE PHOTOGRAPHER WORKING FOR A BLACK NEWSPAPER, GOING INTO EVENTS LIKE JUNETEENTH DAY WHERE YOU COULD BE SEEN AS AN OUTSIDER. WAS THAT EVER AN ISSUE?

BT: Never thought about it. I have been treated so nicely by everybody that I've ever worked with.

KR: TAKING A STEP BACK, YOU GOT YOUR START WITH THE BOYS & GIRLS CLUBS. ARE THERE ANY MEMORIES THAT STAND OUT TO YOU?

BT: That I used to love. They had so many activities, and fortunately a lot of them were on the weekends or at night, because everything was short notice. They would call and say: "We've got to get pictures of this." "We've got to get pictures of that." "Somebody has offered to give us a $25,000 check." "Can you get here and take a picture of them presenting a check?" But the best was at the camp. Camp Whitcomb/Mason—that's the Boys & Girls Clubs camp on Lake Keesus, west of Milwaukee. I think it's still part of the Boys & Girls Clubs. I used to love going out there and photographing the kids. These are kids who are not experienced in lake and outdoor activities, so this was a great experience for them and something I looked forward to every summer.

KR: WE SHOULD TALK ABOUT THE ERNEST LACY INQUEST AND DEMONSTRATIONS. CAN YOU TELL ME WHAT IT WAS LIKE PHOTOGRAPHING THIS INFAMOUS PART OF MILWAUKEE HISTORY?

BT: Apparently, I was thrown out of the courtroom on at least three occasions, but I only recall one. There is a letter that the editor of the Milwaukee Community Journal wrote to Judge Cannon with copies to the district attorney and several other people in regard to the episode. I remember that the Milwaukee Community Journal did not have another photographer in the courtroom, but I'm not certain why. I guess it might be because they asked for credentials and didn't get them. In those days it wasn't cut and dry as to whether you could photograph in the courtroom. I didn't ask for permission, I just went in and started taking pictures. That's when the judge stopped the inquest and took me back into his chambers and mused a long time as to whether I should be allowed to be there. He questioned me extensively. An inquest is a pretty solemn thing, and this was a biggie because there was a lot of community animosity in both ways. When they stopped the inquest in front of a televised audience and the judge made me go back in his chambers, that made an impression. The judge was quite serious. This wasn't a joking matter. I didn't know if he was going to lock me up or what.

KR: OUTSIDE OF THAT, DO YOU HAVE ANY OTHER MEMORIES OF THE INQUEST OR TRIAL, OR OF THE PROTESTS, WHICH YOU ALSO PHOTOGRAPHED?

BT: Oh, sure. I have a photograph at the Milwaukee Art Museum from one of the Lacy protests. It's of Police Chief Harold Breier, when he made the famous statement, "I can go anyplace I want in the City of Milwaukee at any time." He was surrounded by about twenty heavily armed police when he made the statement. And then there's a picture of Wisconsin Avenue with a solid line of police on both sides of the road. When you overlay that with "I can go anyplace I want, anytime I want," ... well, yeah, you can when you're accompanied by twenty cops with rifles and shotguns. The other thing that sticks in my mind is when Harold Breier was called to testify. He was very, very dogmatic that he wasn't going to tell anything to anybody that would do the other side any good. I remember him coming out of the courtroom and looking over at me and saying, "Now, do you know anything you didn't know before?"

KR: I WANTED TO ASK YOU A QUESTION ABOUT A SPECIFIC PHOTO IN THE EXHIBITION. THERE IS A CHILD RUNNING IN FRONT OF THE HELPING HAND PRAYER SERVICE. I WAS CURIOUS IF THAT WAS STAGED?

BT: Oh no. I never staged anything. I just take a picture when I see something that I think will make a good picture. I've photographed a lot of storefront churches and central city churches. I don't know if it's a majority of them or not, but I have many of them.

KR: WHAT IS IT ABOUT THE STOREFRONTS THAT CAPTURES YOUR ATTENTION AND MAKES YOU WANT TO PHOTOGRAPH THEM?

BT: That's probably the influence of some of the old art photographers. There is something about scenes that are pretty routine at the time they were taken, but because of the passage of time have become really interesting.

KR: MOVING ON TO SPORTS, TELL ME ABOUT BASKETBALL. YOU'VE DONE A LOT OF PHOTOGRAPHY OF BUCKS GAMES AND OF MARQUETTE BASKETBALL.

BT: Basketball is the greatest sport in the world for photography, as far as I'm concerned. They feed us well before the game. We always have a nice meal in the media room. You go out and sit down—you have a nice, comfortable seat. They now allow backrests—they didn't in the early years, but we're now allowed to sit on a backrest, so it's quite comfortable. And the action comes to you every twenty seconds. If you miss it, don't worry, they'll be right back. They'll be doing something just as spectacular again. It's the ideal sport. You don't get rained on. It's sixty-five or seventy degrees all the time. Your equipment doesn't get knocked around. It's fun.

KR: CAN YOU TELL ME ABOUT MARQUETTE GAMES IN PARTICULAR?

BT: I've gotten to meet and know so many wonderful people over the years: Players and coaches and band directors. I just got my credentials from Marquette, by the way, to shoot this year's games. I'm looking forward to it.

KR: DO YOU HAVE A FAVORITE MARQUETTE PLAYER TO PHOTOGRAPH, OR A FAVORITE MARQUETTE PLAYER IN GENERAL?

BT: Anyone that does a spectacular play in front of me, that's my favorite player. I want a guy that goes up to the basket and slams the ball through, knocking everybody else out of the way. That's my favorite player, always.

KR: YOU'RE A SPORTS PHOTOGRAPHY FAN.

BT: Sports photography fan. Now you're talking.

KR: IS THERE ANYTHING ELSE YOU'D LIKE TO ADD?

BT: I've met so many interesting people through my work with the Milwaukee Community Journal. Going to weddings of people in the community and being invited to be part of things. It's been wonderful.

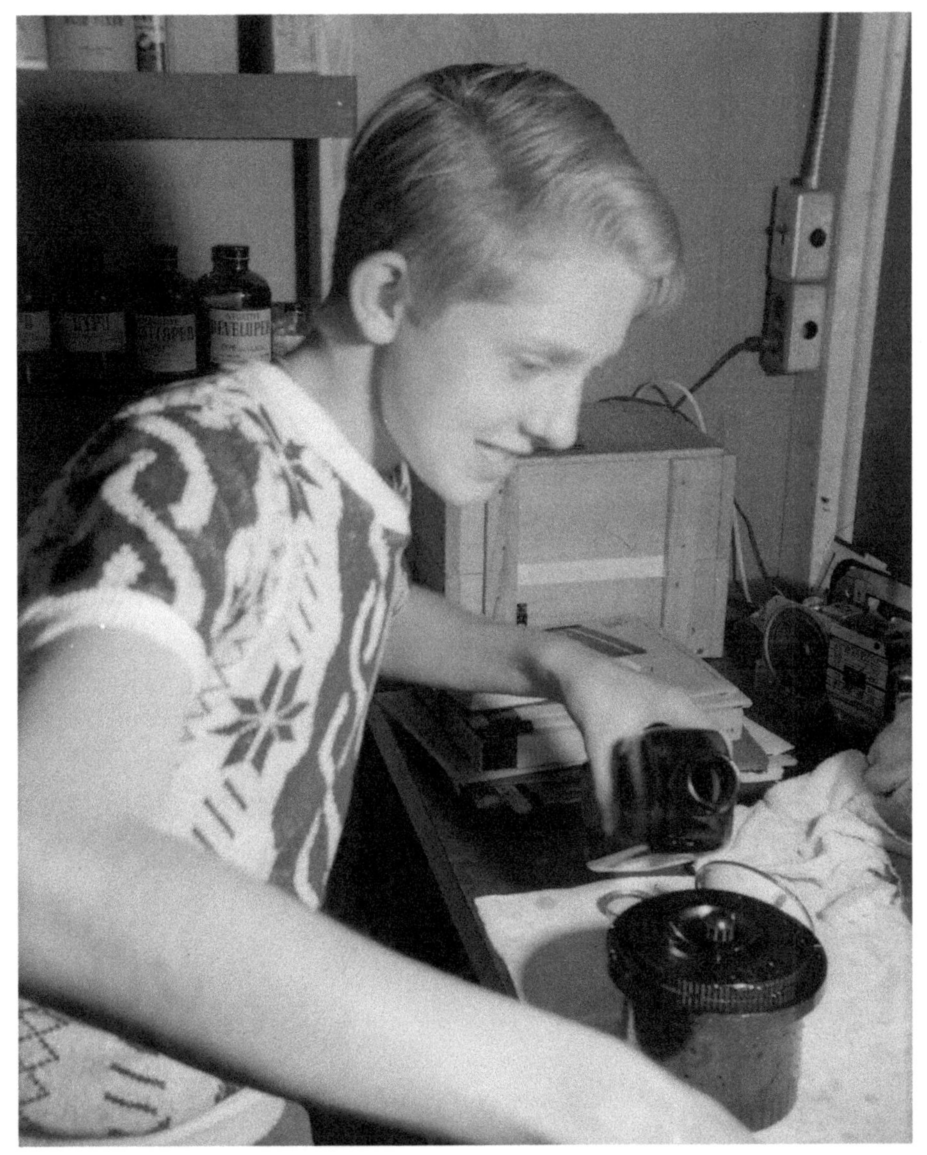

Bill Tennessen in the darkroom, circa 1940s

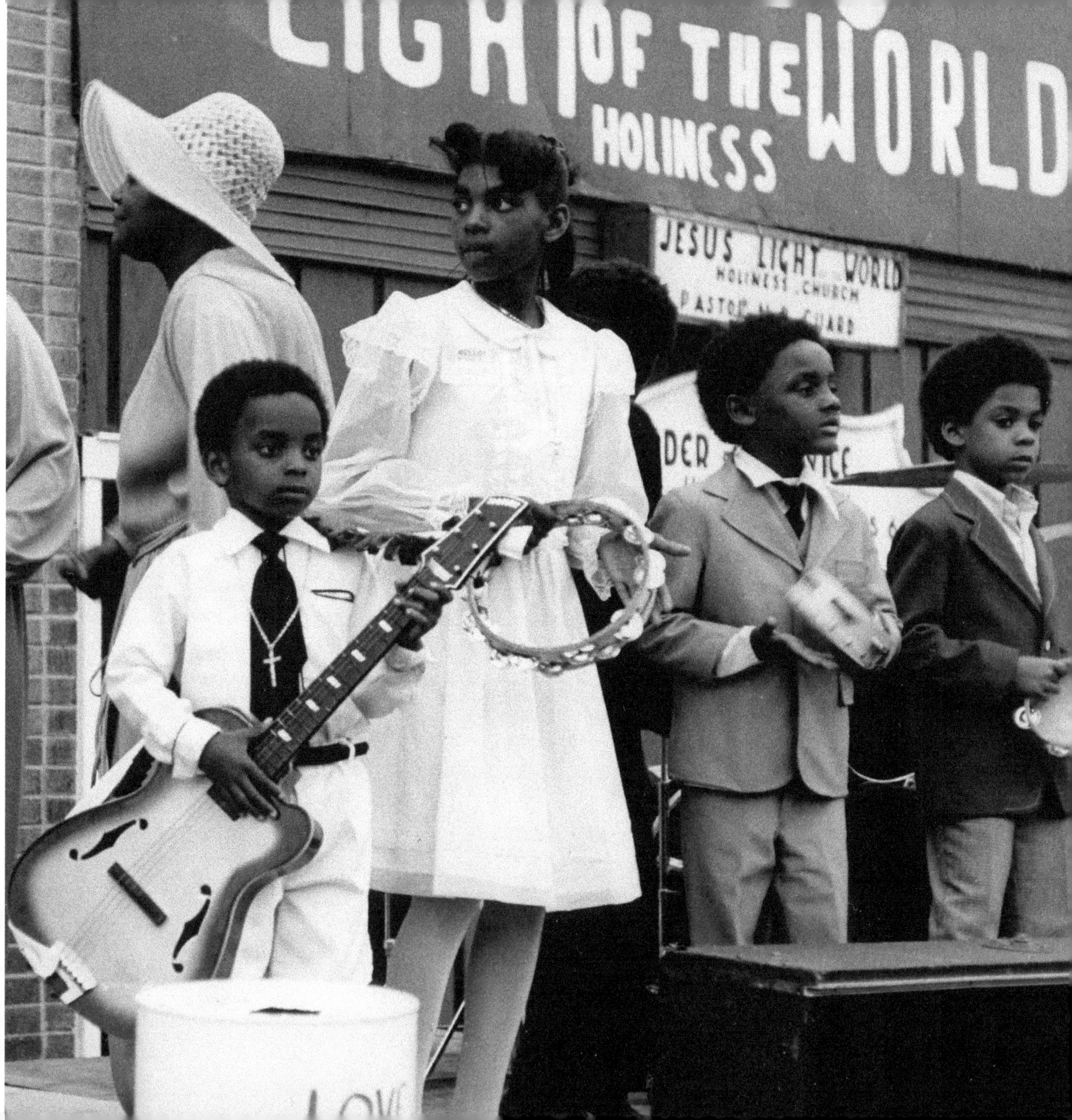

LIGHT OF THE WORLD
HOLINESS
JESUS LIGHT WORLD
HOLINESS CHURCH
PASTOR AND GUARD

Storefront Churches

From traditional African customs to today's diverse denominations, religious and spiritual practices have long played a major role in Black communities. While enslaved, Black people sought solace in their faith and, after abolition, founded their own churches and created new Christian denominations. Church leaders held important roles in the community, particularly during the Civil Rights Movement. Many of Tennessen's photographs reflect the ingenuity and entrepreneurship woven throughout Black communities. Churches have always provided the space for economic and political collectivism, while also nourishing the social and spiritual needs of various communities. Indeed, many storefront churches serve the discrete needs of small-to-moderate-sized congregations, despite facing economic challenges to stay open and afloat.

Going Up Yonder Community Church, 1980s

A woman stands in front of Going Up Yonder Community Church in the 1980s. The pastor of the church was J. L. Martin. Martin and his wife (co-pastor Dianne) continued to run the church out of a different space until his death in 2018.

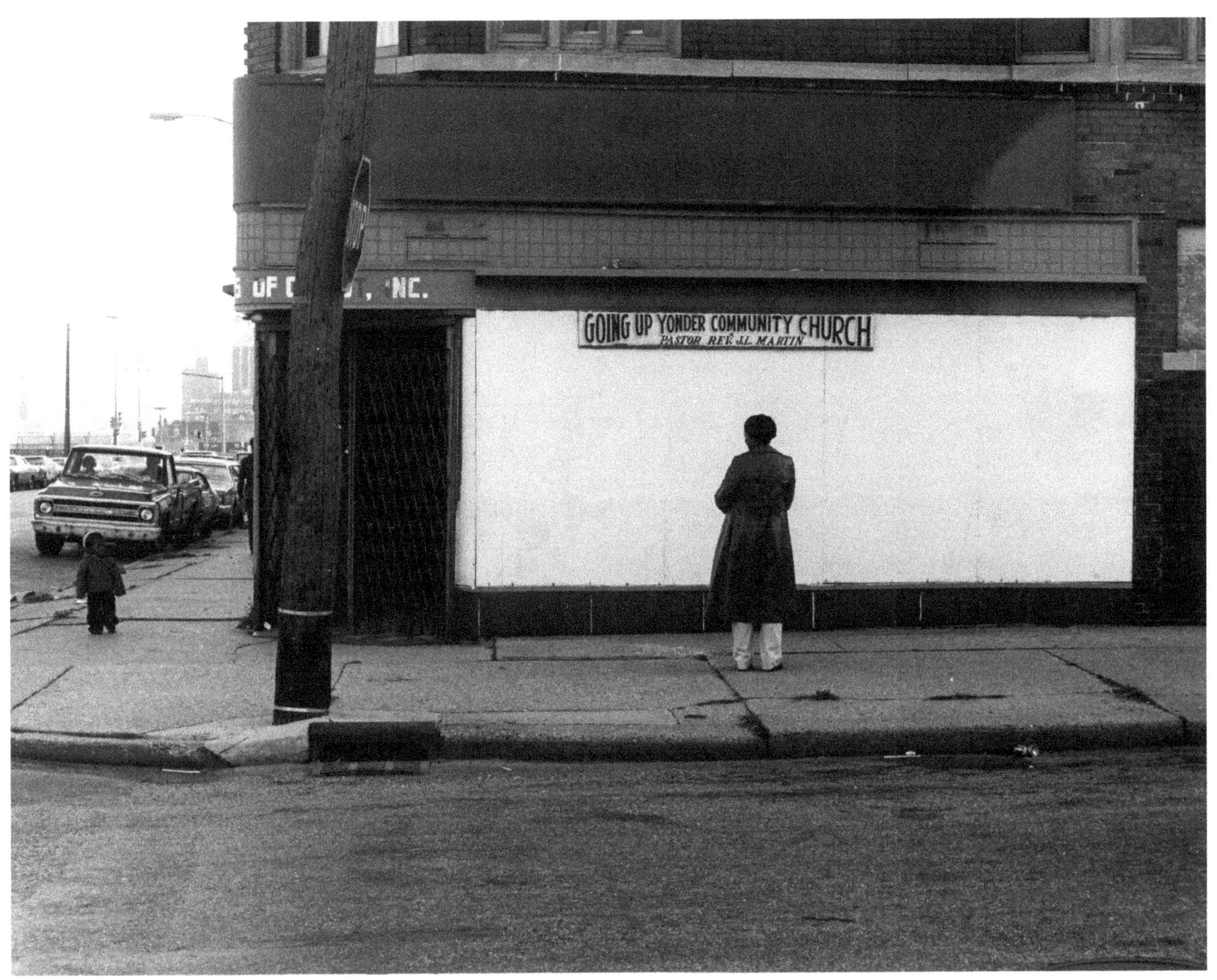
GOING UP YONDER COMMUNITY CHURCH
PASTOR REV. J.L. MARTIN
OF C   T, 'NC.
STOP

Jesus Light of the World, 1980s

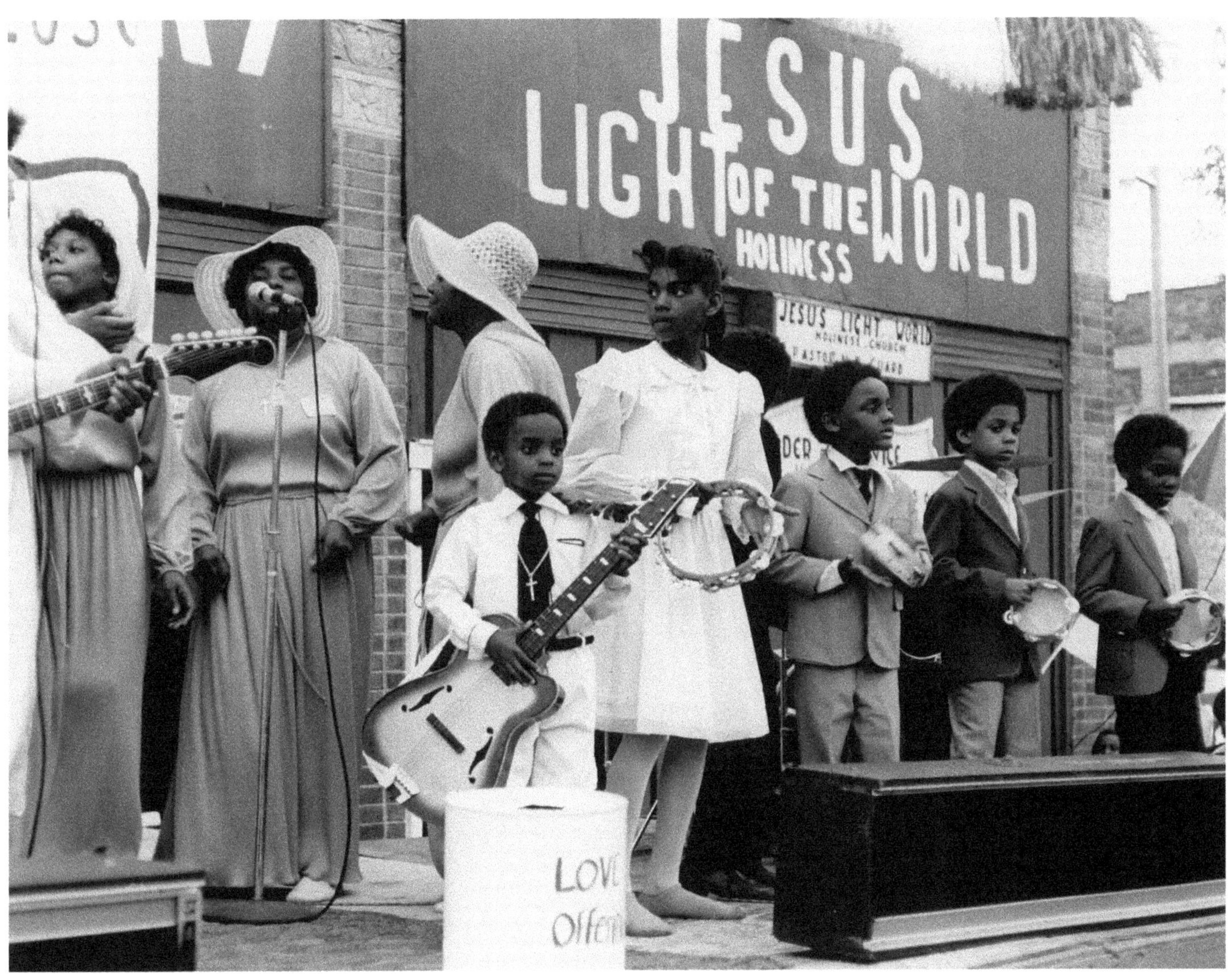
JESUS
LIGHT OF THE WORLD
HOLINESS
JESUS LIGHT WORLD
LOVE
Offer

Helping Hand Church, 1980s

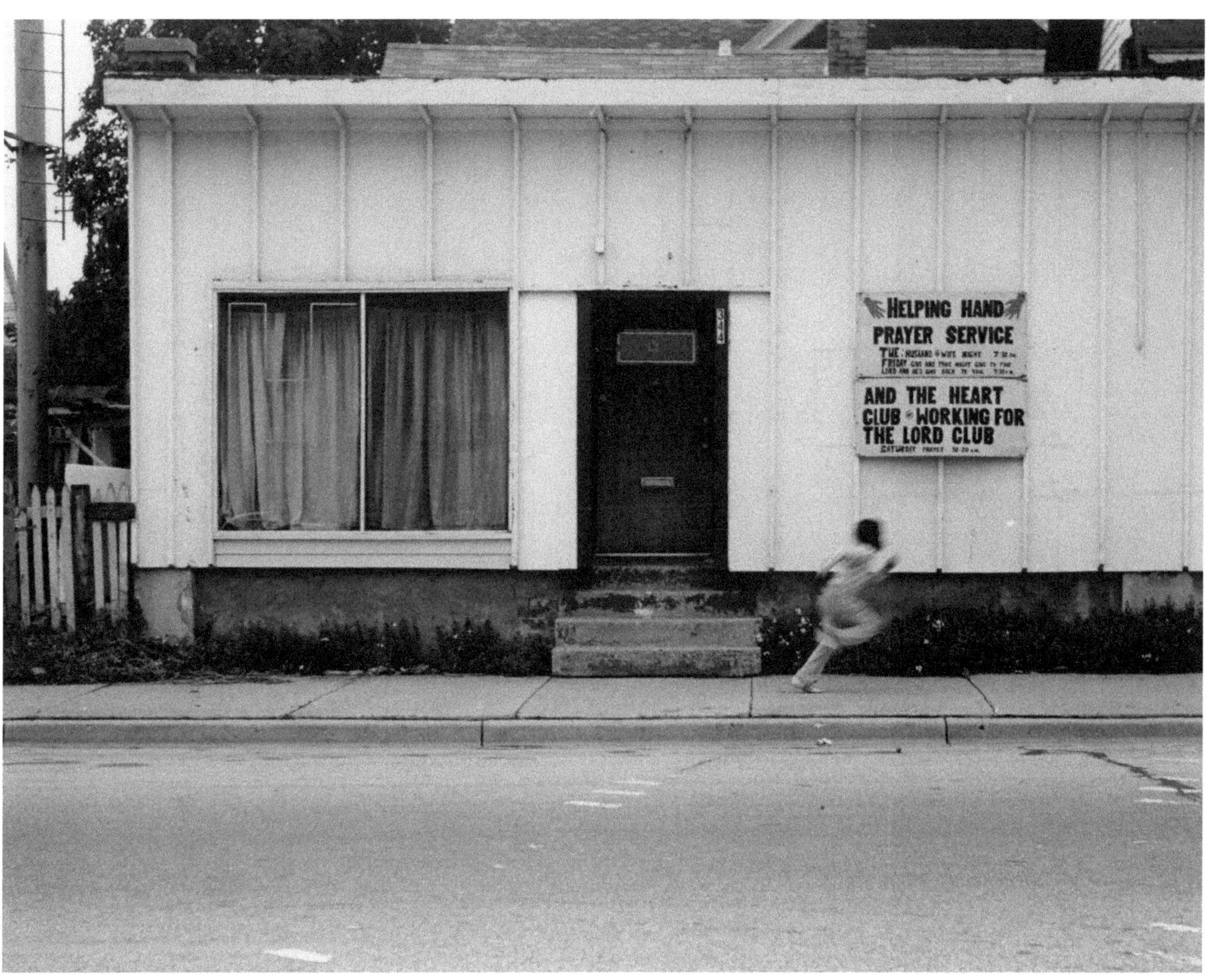
HELPING HAND
PRAYER SERVICE
AND THE HEART
CLUB - WORKING FOR
THE LORD CLUB

Storefront Church and Grocery, 1980s

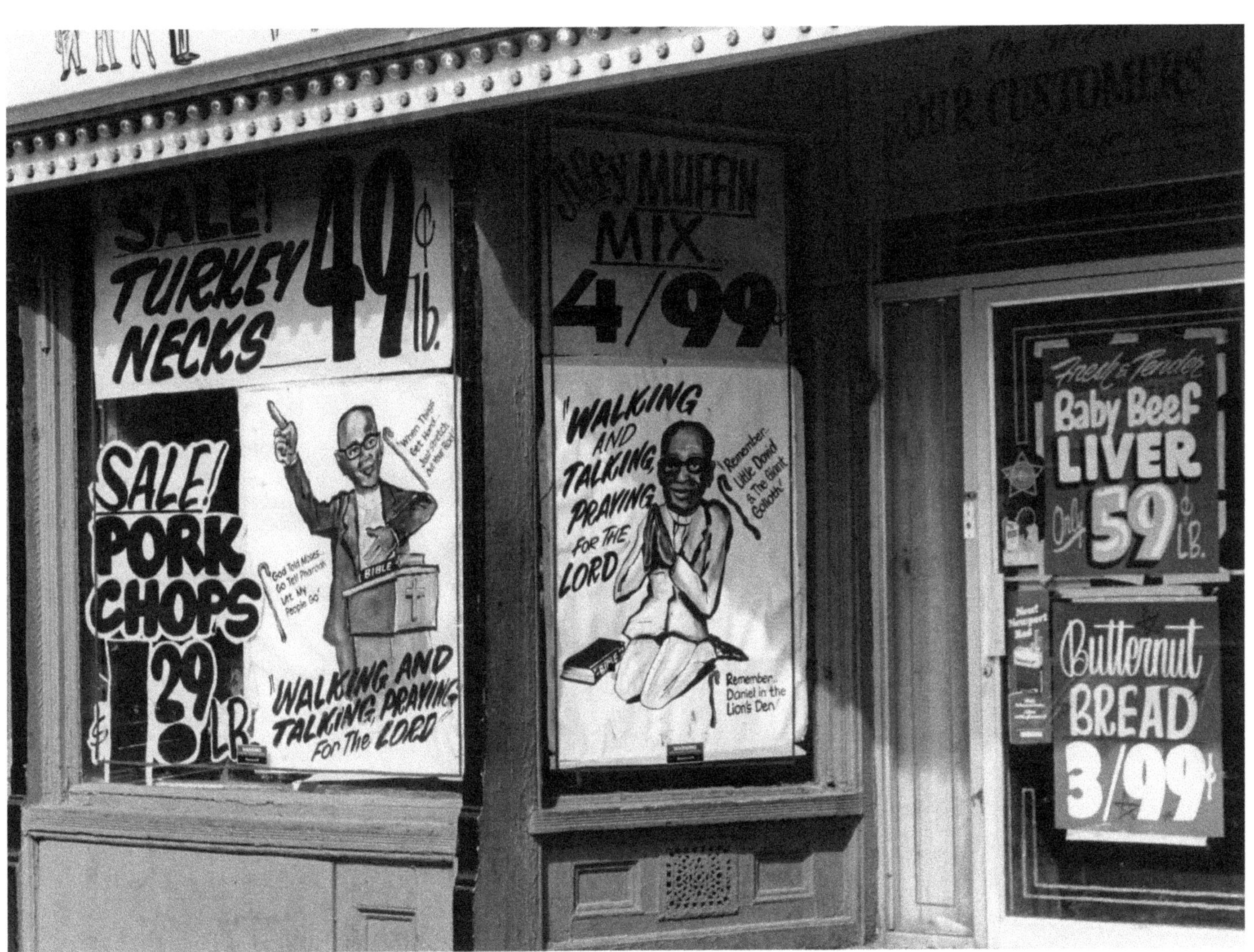

SALE!
TURKEY
NECKS
49¢ lb.
SALE!
PORK
CHOPS
29¢ LB.
BIBLE
God Told Moses... Go Tell Pharrah Let My People Go!
When They Get Hard Nar-stretch Out Hair Boy
"WALKING AND TALKING, PRAYING For The LORD"
MUFFIN
MIX
4/99¢
"WALKING AND TALKING, PRAYING FOR THE LORD"
Remember... Little David & The Giant Goliath
Remember... Daniel in the Lion's Den
OUR CUSTOMERS
Fresh & Tender
BABY BEEF
LIVER
Only 59¢ LB.
Butternut
BREAD
3/99¢

Revival Center at Third and Juneau, 1984

The Revival Center, created by Prophet Blackmon, was located within the Sydney HiH building at Third and Juneau. Blackmon's center served as more than just a church; it held rummage sales and offered laundry and tailoring services. Like many of Sydney HiH's storefronts in the late 20th century, the Revival Center did not last long. Blackmon received an eviction notice for the space in 1985.

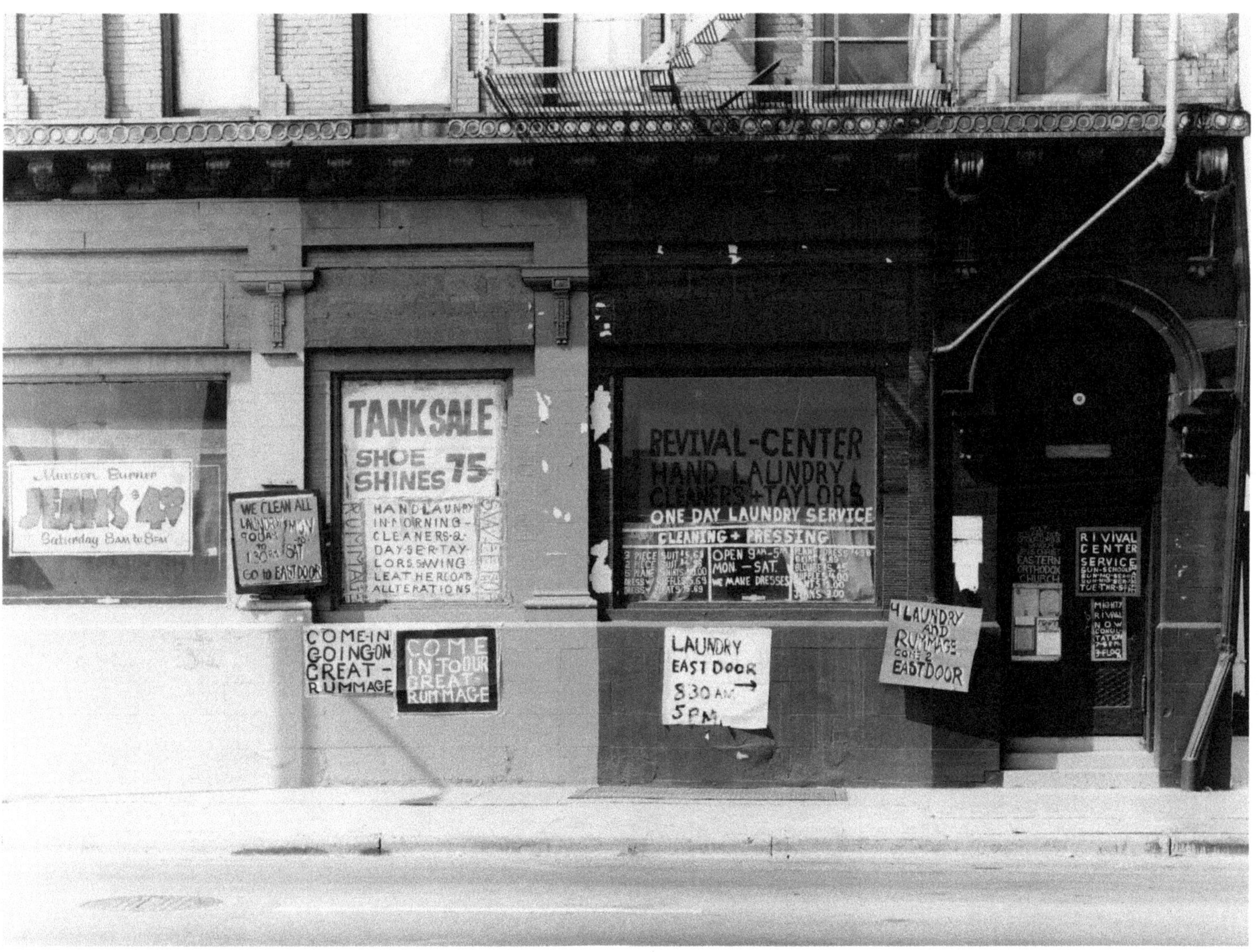

Munson Burner
JEANS '49
Saturday 8am to 8pm
TANK SALE
SHOE SHINES 75
WE CLEAN ALL
LAUNDRY
9:00 AM
TO
1:30 PM SAT
GO to EAST DOOR
HAND LAUNDRY
IN MORNING
CLEANERS &
DAY SER TAY
LORS SEWING
LEATHER COAT
ALLTERATIONS
RUMMAGE
COME IN
GOING ON
GREAT
RUMMAGE
COME
IN TO OUR
GREAT
RUMMAGE
REVIVAL-CENTER
HAND LAUNDRY
CLEANERS + TAYLORS
ONE DAY LAUNDRY SERVICE
CLEANING + PRESSING
OPEN 9 AM - 5 PM
MON. — SAT.
WE MAKE DRESSES
LAUNDRY
EAST DOOR
8:30 AM
5 PM
4 LAUNDRY
AND
RUMMAGE
COME 2
EAST DOOR
EASTERN
ORTHODOX
CHURCH
RIVIVAL
CENTER
SERVICE
SUN SCHOOL
MIGHTY
RIVIVAL
NOW

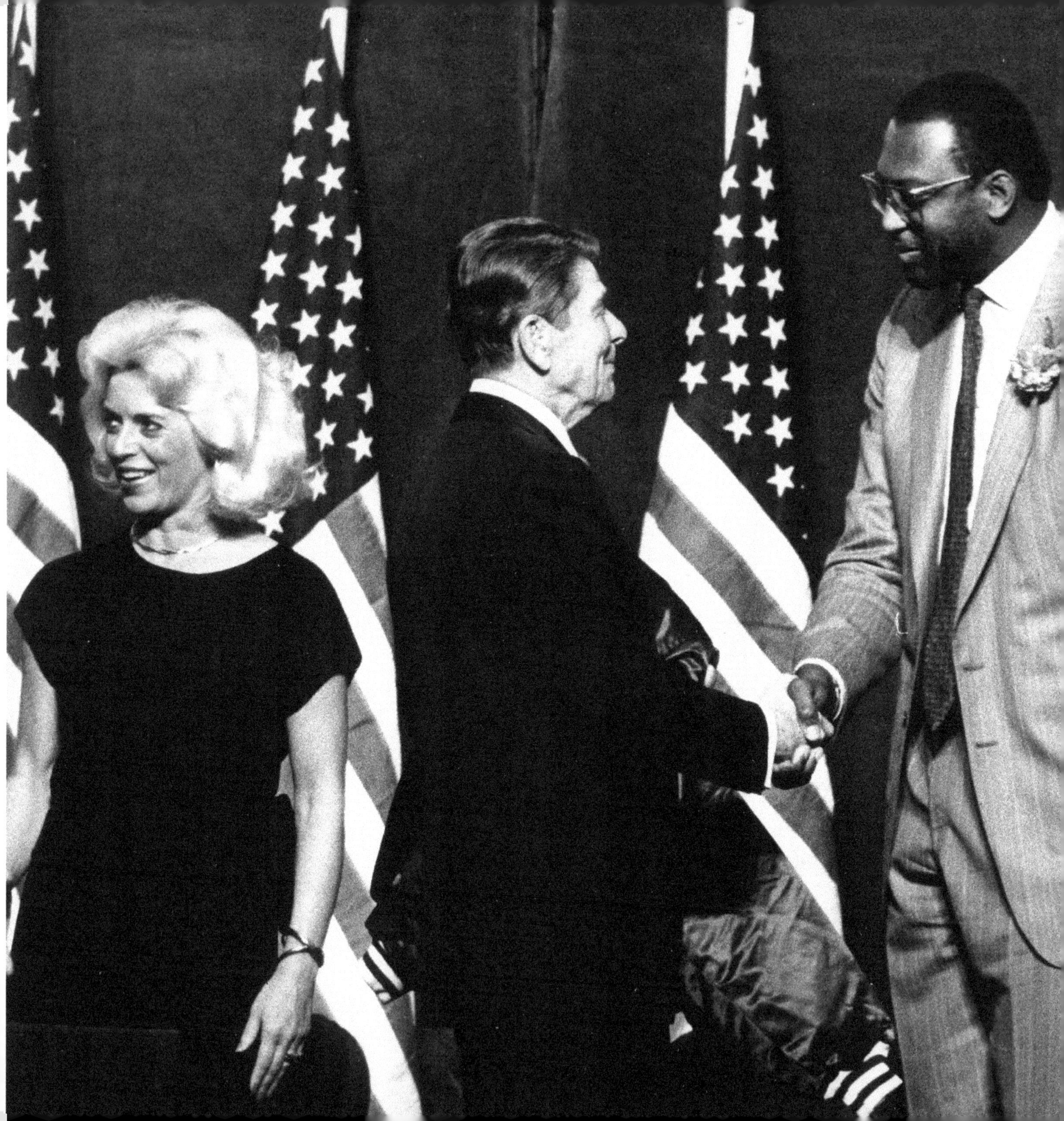

Politicians/VIPs

Throughout the 1980s and 1990s, Bill Tennessen documented visits to Milwaukee by some of the most influential politicians of the time: Bill and Hillary Clinton, Jimmy Carter, Ronald Reagan, and Jesse Jackson among them.

Following the Voting Rights Act of 1965, Black leaders throughout the country continued to push for greater representation in political offices, from city councils to congressional seats. In the 1970s and 1980s, Shirley Chisholm and Jesse Jackson ran major presidential campaigns and received a surprising number of primary votes, demonstrating the power of their messages and the impact of removing barriers that prevented African Americans from voting in many states. Prominent local politicians and changemakers of this time, including Vel R. Phillips (who drafted Milwaukee's fair housing legislation), Lloyd Barbee (president of the Wisconsin NAACP, who fought to end segregation in Milwaukee schools) and Dr. James Cameron (founder of America's Black Holocaust Museum), raised awareness of key concerns on behalf of Black Milwaukeeans.

The work and messages of these visionaries, activists, politicians, and scholars were recognized and conveyed by the Milwaukee Community Journal and other Black news outlets and preserved for history through Tennessen's lens.

***Alderwoman Vel R. Phillips, Dr. Winston Van Horne, and Alderwoman
Marlene Johnson-Odom, 1983***
Print from digital scan

Vel R. Phillips was a trailblazing figure in Wisconsin history. She was an accomplished attorney, judge, alderperson, and lauded civil rights leader, and she served as secretary of state from 1979 to 1983. Phillips was the first African American woman to receive a degree from the University of Wisconsin Law School, the first African American and first woman to be elected alderwoman to the Milwaukee Common Council and the first African American and woman jurist in Wisconsin. In the fall of 1983, she served as an adjunct professor at the University of Wisconsin–Milwaukee, teaching in the African and African Diaspora Studies program. Phillips is pictured with the department chair, Winston Van Horne, and Milwaukee Alderwoman Marlene Johnson-Odom.

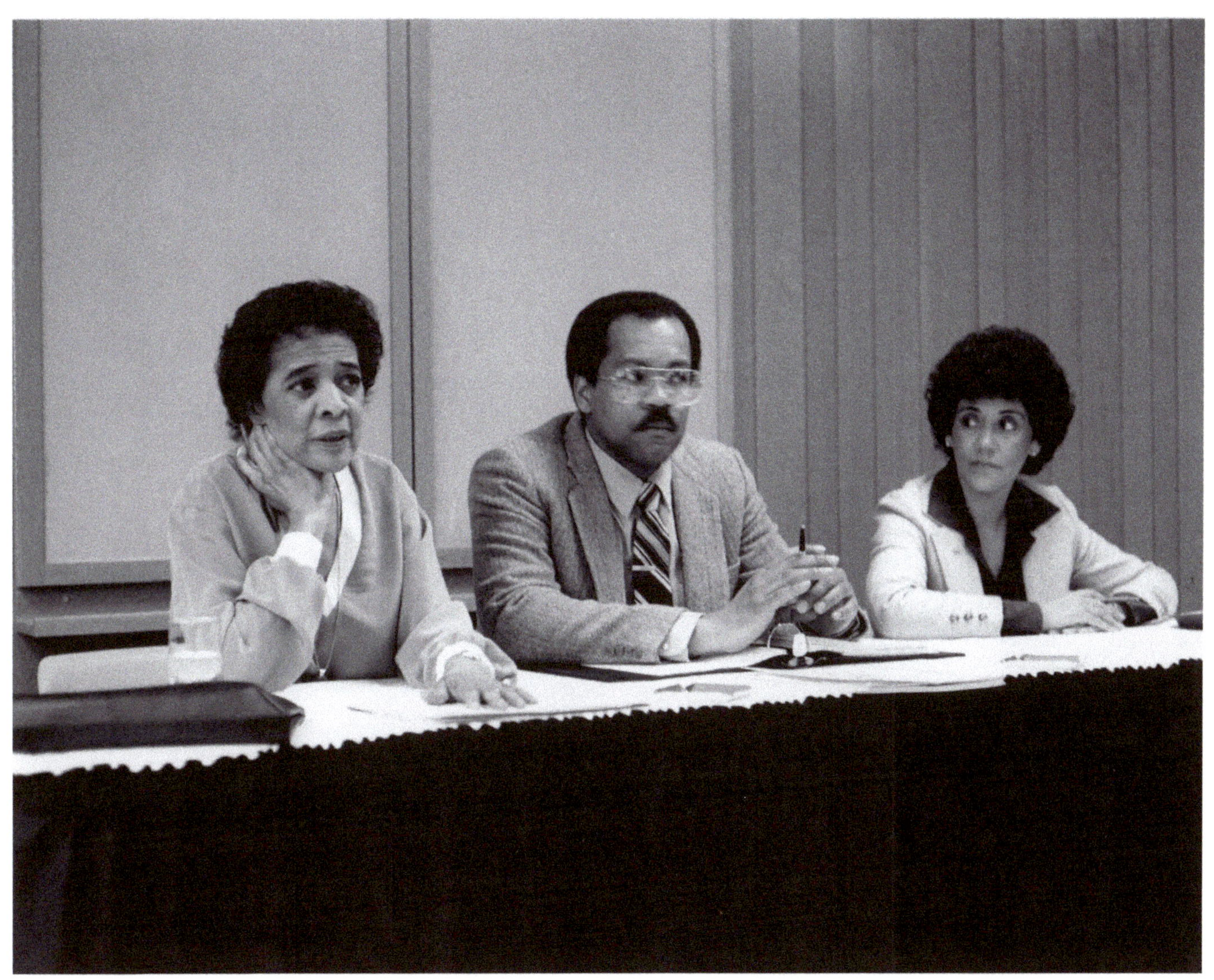

Coretta Scott King and Marcia P. Coggs at Marquette University, 1983
Print from digital scan

Coretta Scott King (left) and Marcia P. Coggs (right) at an event at Marquette University in 1983. Women played an important role in the Civil Rights Movement, despite often being overshadowed by their male counterparts. King is famously known as the widow of Martin Luther King Jr., but her own activism began before their marriage and continued long after Dr. King's death. In 1983 alone, she successfully advocated for the creation of a holiday in her late husband's honor, formed the Coalition of Conscience (more than 800 human rights organizations that sponsored the 20th anniversary of the March on Washington), and moved to have members of the LGBTQIA+ community be considered protected under the Civil Rights Act. Milwaukee native Marcia P. Coggs was an activist in her own right as the head of a prominent political family and the first African American woman elected to the Wisconsin State Assembly (in 1976), where she was known for her focus on creating equal opportunities.

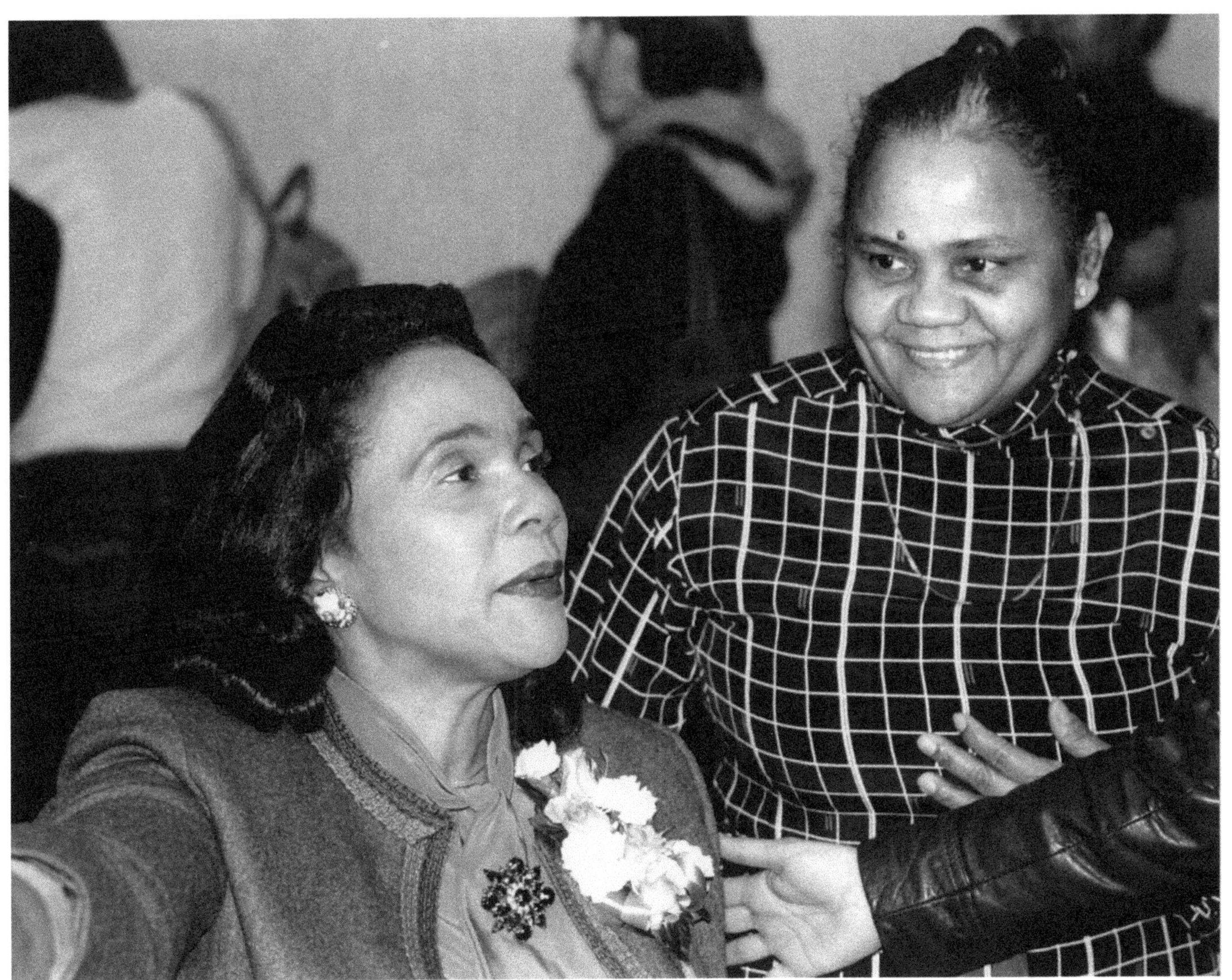

Senator Bob Kasten, Elizabeth "Bo" Black, President Reagan,
and Bob Lanier at the Milwaukee Convention Center, 1985

President Ronald Reagan is guest of honor at a fundraising dinner for major donors supporting the reelection of Senator Robert Kasten. Here he shakes hands with Milwaukee Bucks player and future Hall of Famer Bob Lanier. To Reagan's left is Summerfest director Elizabeth "Bo" Black. Kasten won the Senate seat against Ed Garvey in a contentious election.

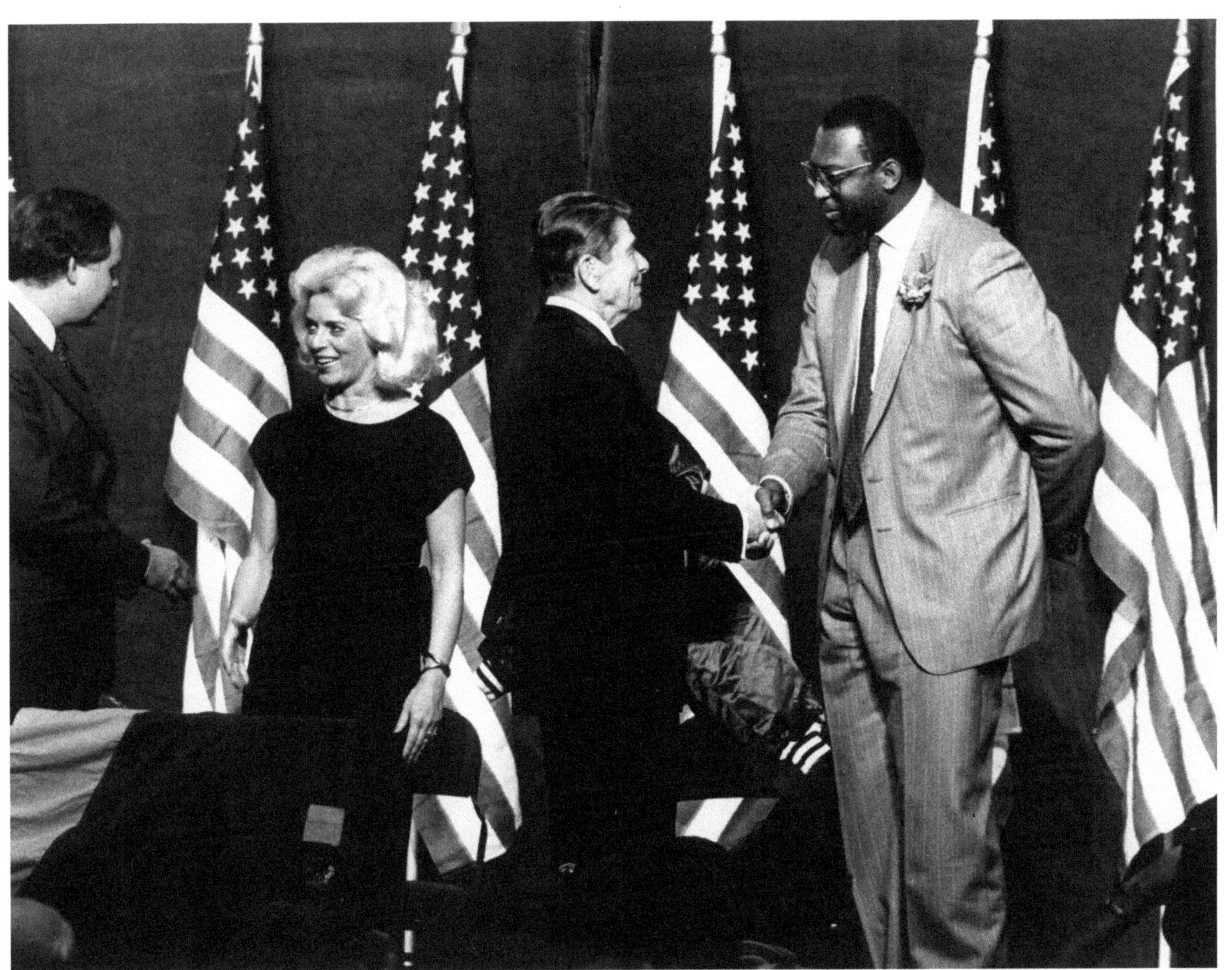

Rev. Jesse Jackson at the Milwaukee Press Club, 1986

During both of his bids for the presidency in the 1980s, Rev. Jesse Jackson held a number of events in Milwaukee in hope of gaining the support of the city's delegates. On February 24, 1986, Jackson visited the Milwaukee Press Club to take part in the long-standing tradition of adding to their signatures collection. Currently, most of the over 1,200 signed plaques in the collection are housed at the archives at the University of Wisconsin–Milwaukee. A number of autographs, including Jackson's, are on permanent loan to the Milwaukee Press Club and are on display at the club's Newsroom Pub.

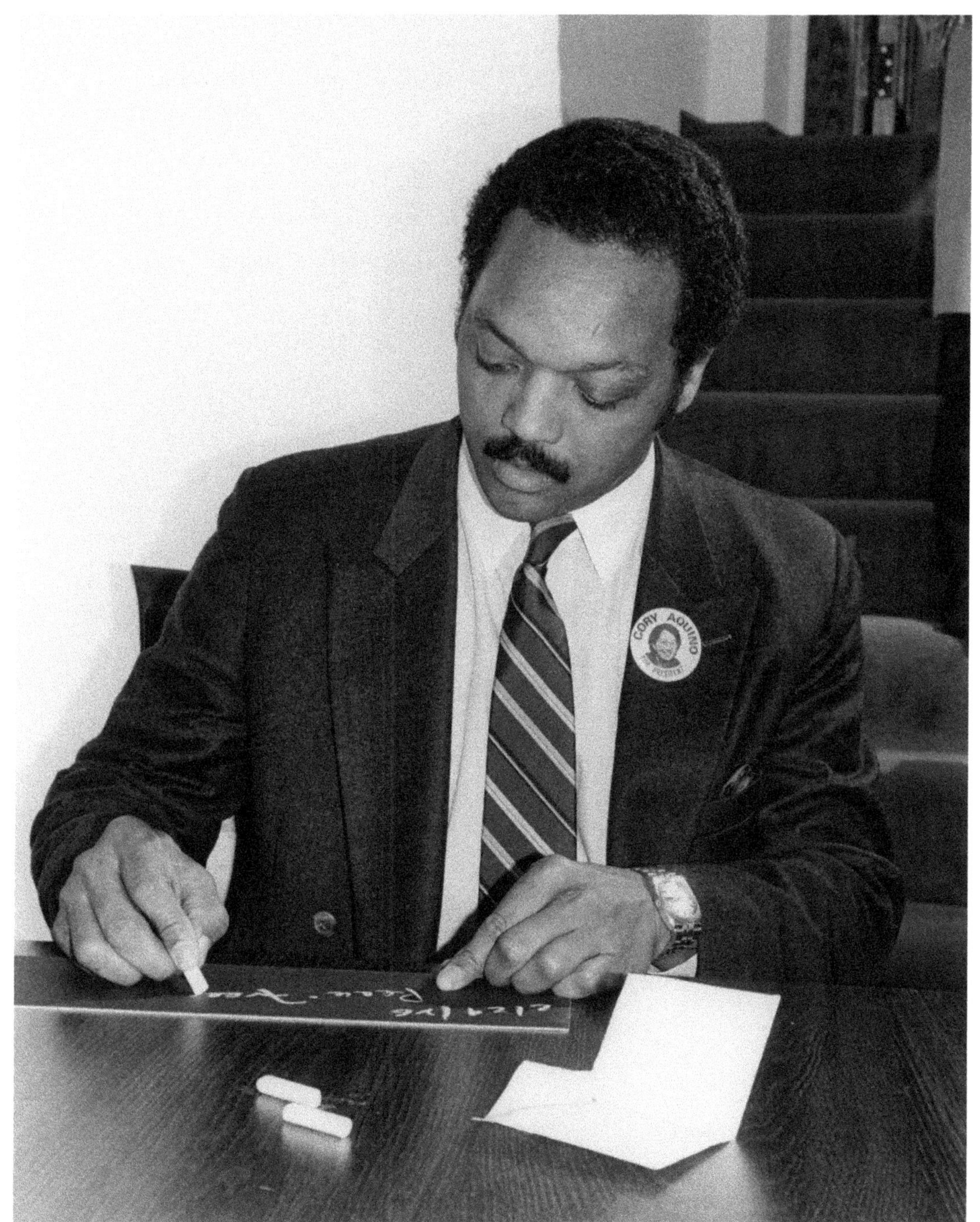

President Jimmy Carter at Habitat for Humanity, 1989

Former President Jimmy Carter greets neighbors at a construction site for Habitat for Humanity on June 13, 1989. Carter was in Milwaukee to head up a weeklong project that involved the building of six new homes near 23rd and Walnut, and the renovation of eight other houses near 34rd and Garfield. The yearly Carter Work Project was a collaboration between Jimmy and Rosalynn Carter and Habitat for Humanity that began in 1984 and continues to this day.

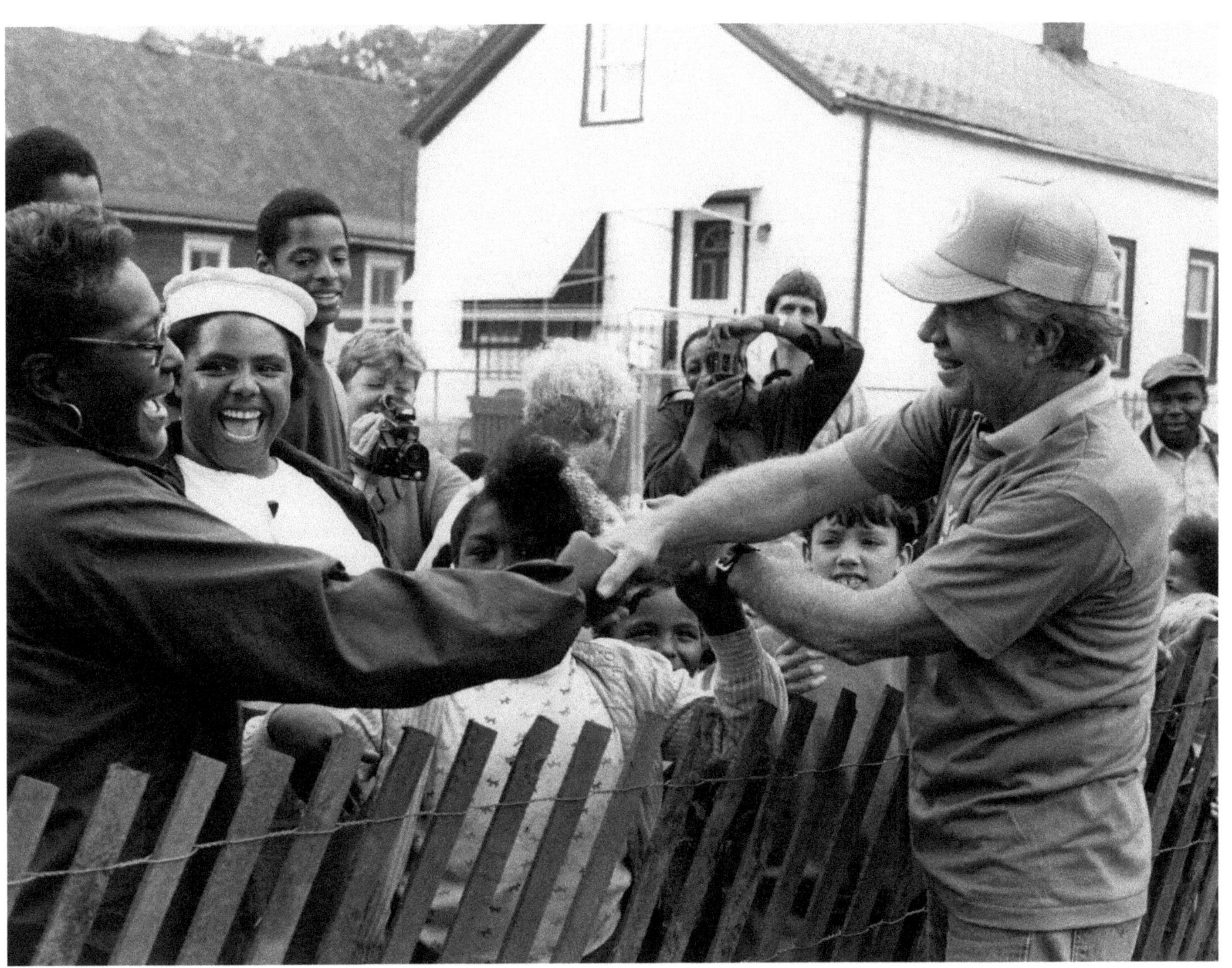

Dr. Joe William Trotter Jr. (left) and Dr. James Cameron (right) spoke at the Wisconsin Humanities Committee Conference "The Stories We Tell" at the Park East Hotel in Milwaukee on May 29, 1991. Dr. Trotter, a professor of history at Carnegie Mellon University and author of Black Milwaukee, gave the event's keynote address. Dr. Cameron, a scholar, activist, and lynching survivor, established America's Black Holocaust Museum in Milwaukee's Bronzeville neighborhood in 1988.

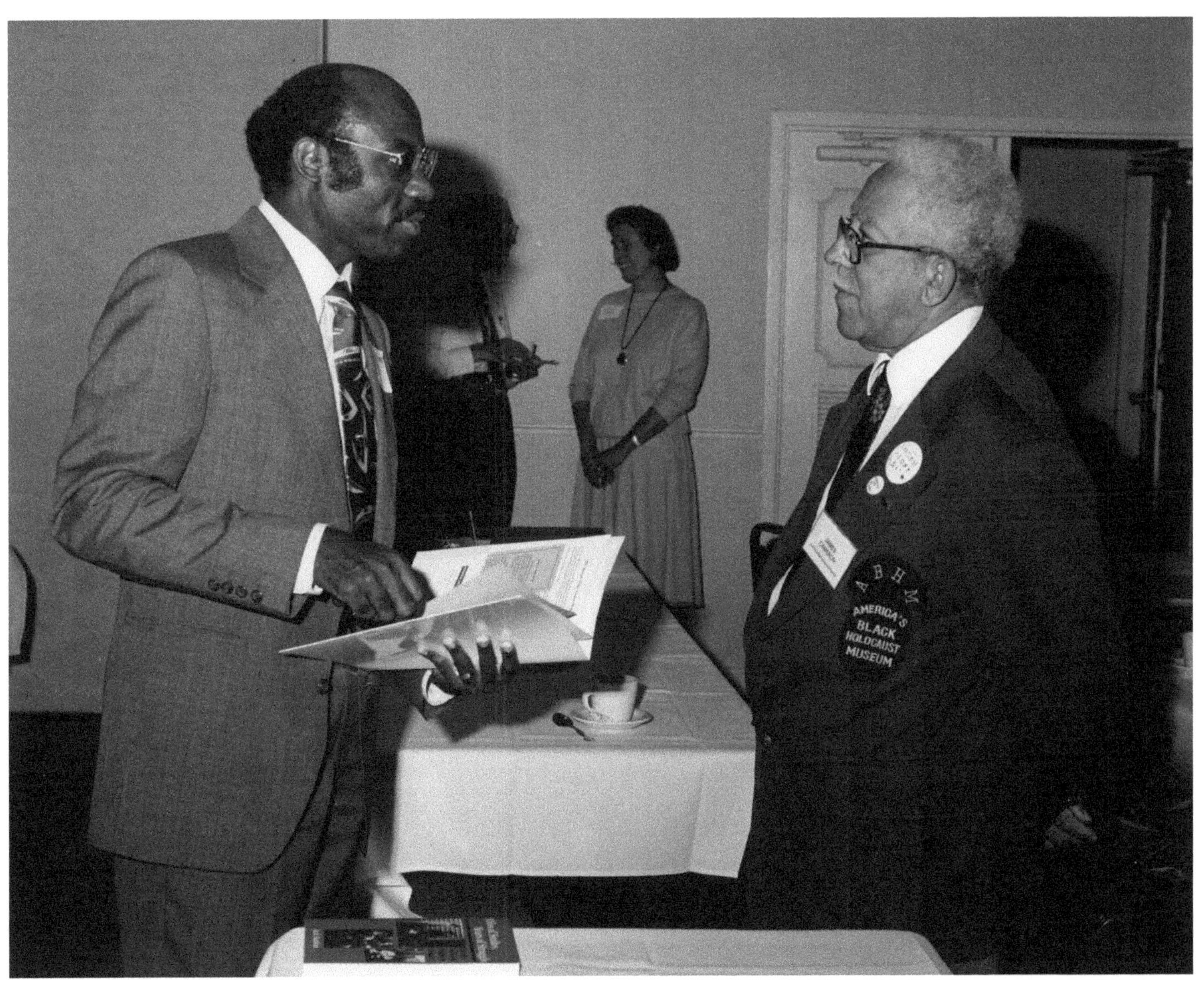
A B H M
AMERICA'S
BLACK
HOLOCAUST
MUSEUM

**_Sheriff Richard Artison, Congressman Jim Moody, Hillary Clinton,
Bill Clinton, and Senator Herb Kohl, 1992_**

On October 20, 1992, the Clinton campaign held a rally at the Wisconsin Center as part of its final push to the November 3 election. Presidential hopeful Bill Clinton was joined on stage by his wife, Hillary, Jim Moody (the U.S. representative for Wisconsin's Fifth District), and Milwaukee County Sheriff Richard Artison. All watched as Senator Herb Kohl spoke.

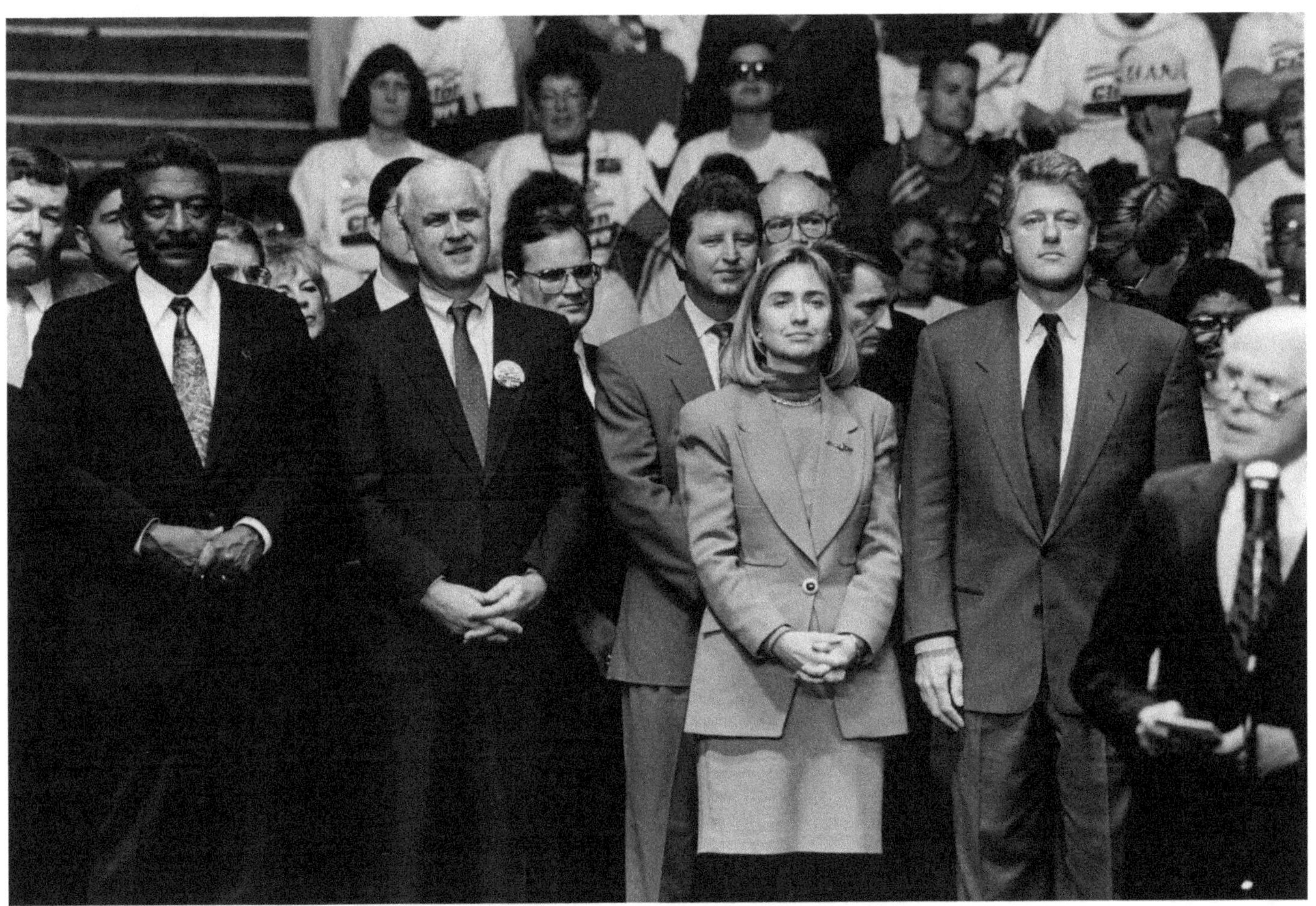

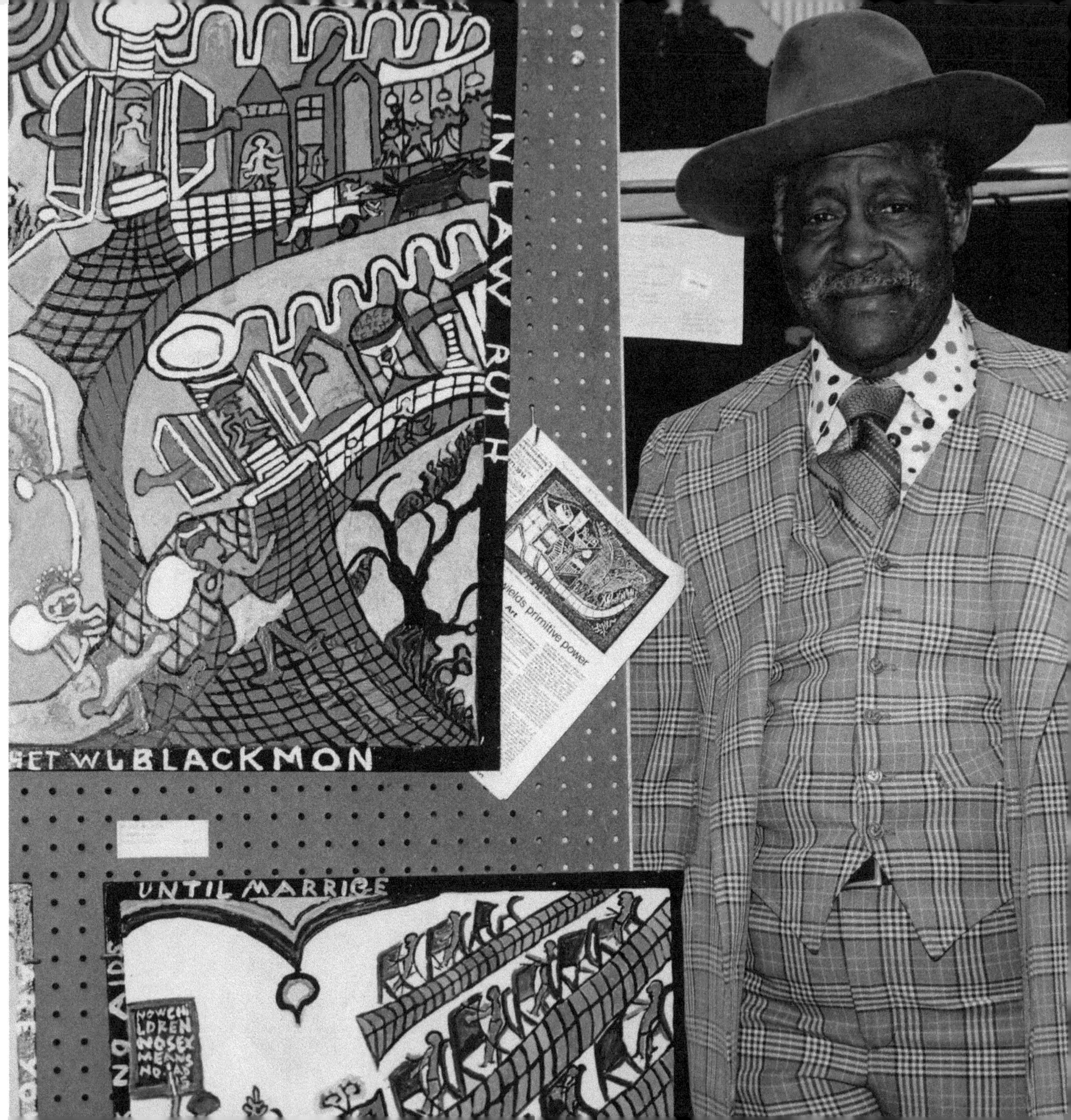
IN LAW WROTH
yields primitive power
Art
GET WL BLACKMON
UNTIL MARRIGE
NO CHILDREN NO SEX MEANS NO AIDS

The Arts

Milwaukee's Black community boasts a proud and rich history of visual and performing arts, literature, and architecture. From the sultry sounds of Al Jarreau, to the provocative filmmaking of John Ridley, to the powerful impact of hip-hop culture, Milwaukee's art scene is a beacon for community collectivism and one of the main ingredients informing African American identity and self-determination.

Art also provides the spiritual sustenance to generate cultural and political movements that confront racism and issues of inequality. Indeed, art and artists expose injustices that demand our heartfelt attention and bring forth imaginings of a democratic future.

Bill Tennessen's photographs document a variety of Milwaukee arts, including local murals and Ko-Thi Dance Company performances.

Artist Reynaldo Hernandez with His Design for the Inner City Arts Council Community Mural Project, 1984

The Inner City Arts Council (ICAC) was established in 1968 on the corner of Seventh Street and North Avenue. In 1984, Reynaldo Hernandez created the mural Celebrate the Arts that adorns the west facade of the building. It was painted by youth from the Milwaukee Commando Project to celebrate the proliferation of the arts in the community. Highlighting African and African American art and artists, the mural includes images of the Mask of Benin and Miles Davis, as well as a self-portrait of the artist. According to Hernandez, "All the different art forms that we have in our soul is on the wall—music, dance, theater, and history." Celebrate the Arts was restored in 2015.

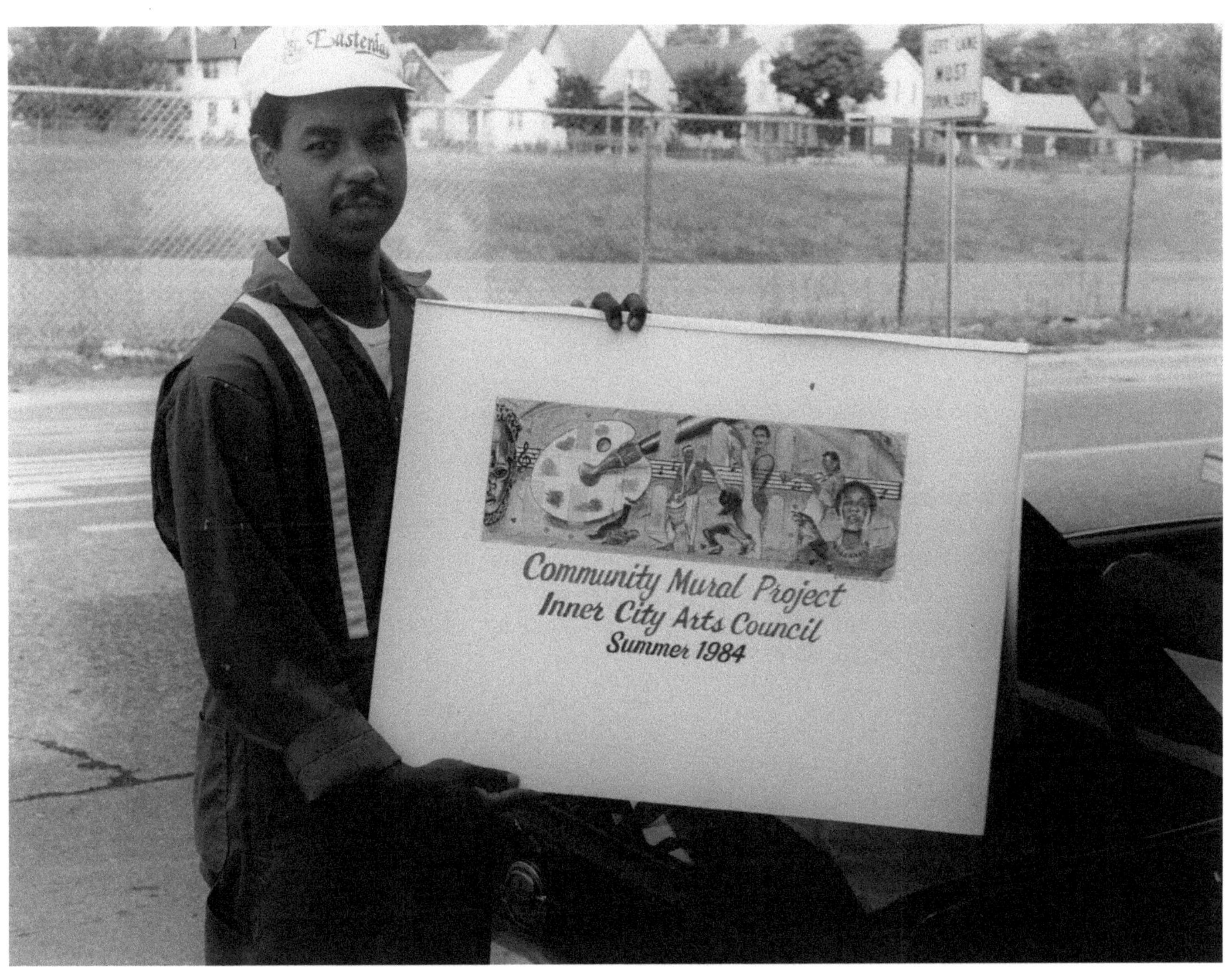
Community Mural Project
Inner City Arts Council
Summer 1984

Prophet William J. Blackmon at the Inner-City Arts Festival, 1989

Prophet William J. Blackmon poses with three of his works at the Inner-City Arts Festival in 1989. Before taking up his calling as an artist and prophet, Blackmon was a business owner and shoe repairman. Merging the spiritual with the secular, he preached from his shoe repair shop and revival center, located in the Sydney HiH building at Third and Juneau. His preaching took the form of colorful paintings focusing on Christian subject matter to share his message of faith and healing. It was through these painted advertisements on his storefront windows that Blackmon's career as an artist began.

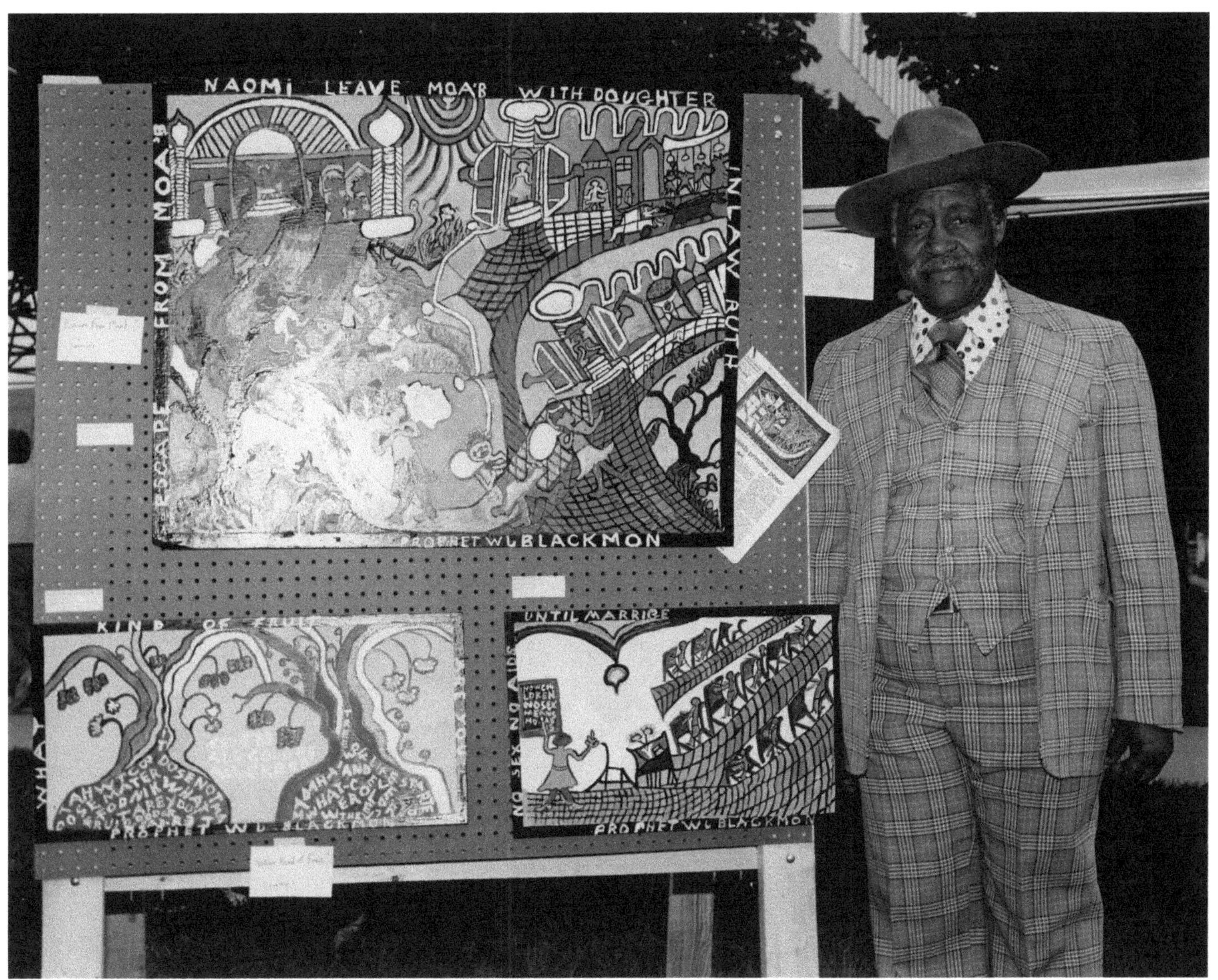

NAOMI LEAVE MOA'B WITH DOUGHTER IN LAW RUTH
ESCAPE FROM MOA'B
PROPHET WL BLACKMON
KIND OF FRUIT
PROPHET WL BLACKMON
UNTIL MARRICE
NO SEX NO AIDS
PROPHET WL BLACKMON

Ko-Thi Dance Company's 20th Anniversary Celebration
at the Pabst Theater, 1989

A dancer jumps before a drumline guided by music director and drummer Dumah Saafir during a performance celebrating Ko-Thi Dance Company's 20th anniversary. "Ko-Thi" in Sherbro (a language of Sierra Leone) means "go black." The company was founded in 1969 by Ferne Caulker-Bronson. Honoring both traditional and modern African dance, Caulker's goal was to lessen the disconnect between Africans and African Americans by embracing cultural heritage as a form of empowerment. Caulker has since become a seminal figure in bringing African dance to Wisconsin. She was the first person to implement African dance classes at the University of Wisconsin–Milwaukee and to build a degree program that specializes in African dance. Since Ko-Thi's founding, African dance has flourished as an art form in Wisconsin and across the country.

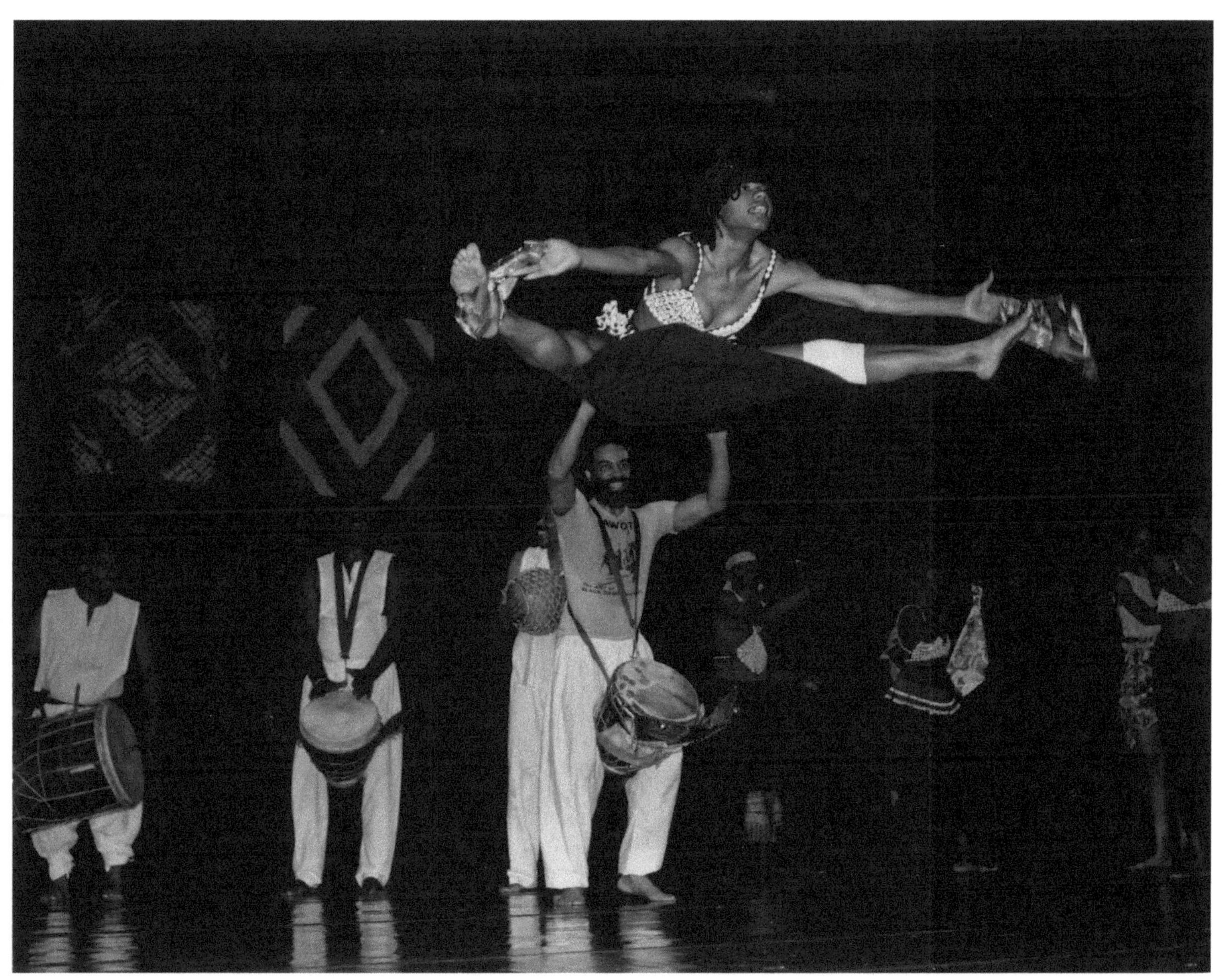

Mural Painting—Commissioned by the Boys & Girls Clubs of Greater Milwaukee, 1991

Once located at Sixth and Walnut, this mural, painted by George Gist, was commissioned by the Boys & Girls Clubs of Greater Milwaukee in 1991 to celebrate the performing arts. Gist, a Detroit native who created 300 murals during his lifetime, painted 20 murals in Milwaukee, including one at 31st and Brown that celebrates the efforts of the Wisconsin Black Cowboys and Buffalo Soldiers Association.

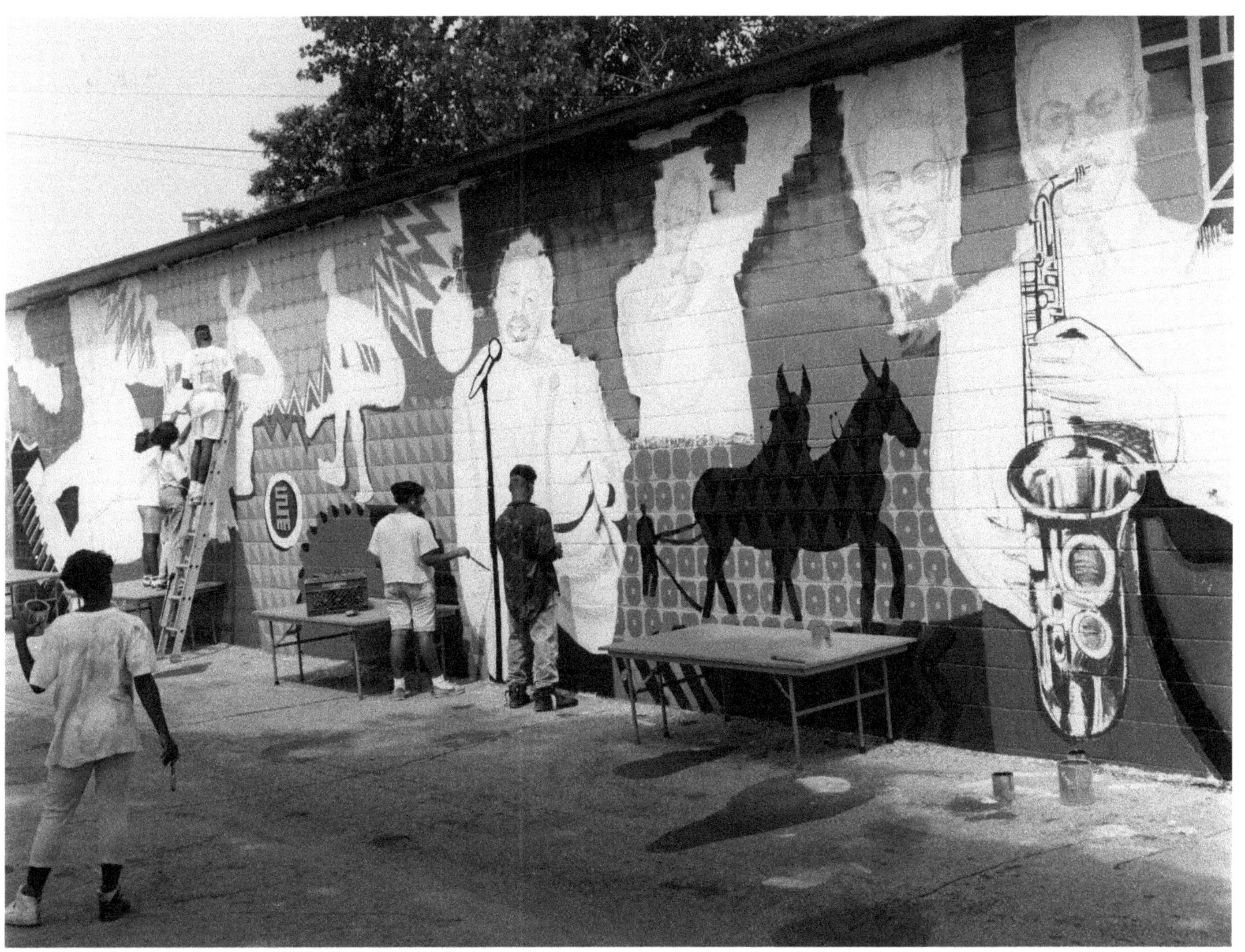

The Patchwork Mural by Ras 'Ammar Nsoroma,
at 430 W. North Avenue, 1991

The Patchwork mural, located one block from America's Black Holocaust Museum, weaves local Black history with the African American tradition of quilt making. Quilting preserves Black history by passing stories from generation to generation. With funding from a City of Milwaukee grant, local artist Ras 'Ammar Nsoroma and youth from the O. C. White Soul Club completed the mural in the summer of 1991. Held up by elders on each side, the central quilt pattern, with colorful star motifs, depicts an array of Black community leaders. Retouched in 2012, the mural continues to garner interest. It recently inspired the "Gathering Place" uniform released by the Milwaukee Bucks in 2022.

According to Nsoroma, there was an elder who sat on her porch across the street each day and watched as he painted the mural. He used her likeness as a model for the female elder holding up the quilt. She attended the mural dedication and was introduced along with some of the other dignitaries.

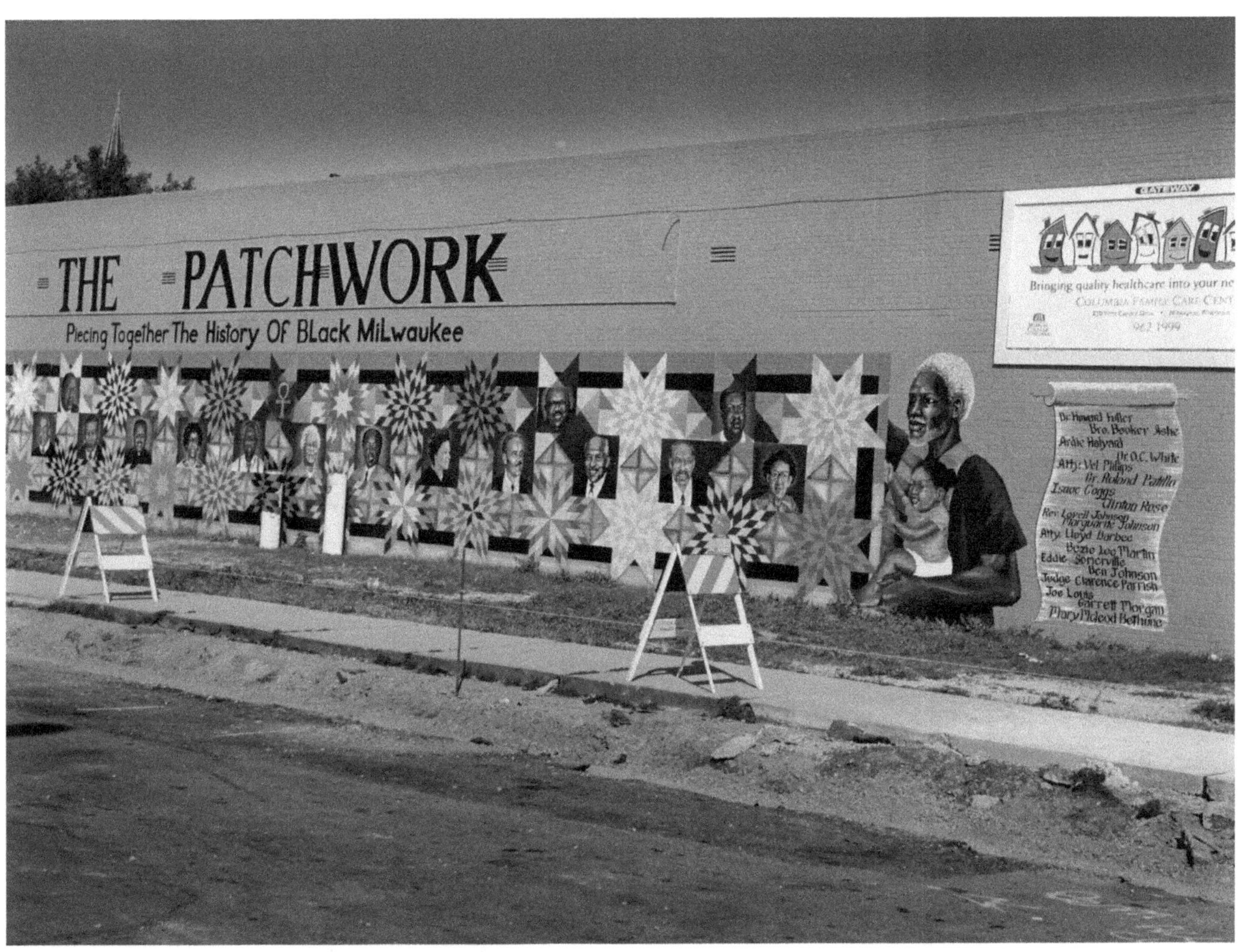
THE PATCHWORK
Piecing Together The History Of Black Milwaukee
GATEWAY
Bringing quality healthcare into your ne
COLUMBIA FAMILY CARE CENT
962-1999
Dr. Howard Fuller
Bro. Booker Ashe
Ardie Halyard
Dr. O.C. White
Atty. Vel Phillips
Dr. Roland Pattillo
Isaac Coggs
Clinton Rose
Rev. Lovell Johnson
Marguerite Johnson
Atty. Lloyd Barbee
Bessie Lee Martin
Eddie Somerville
Ben Johnson
Judge Clarence Parrish
Joe Louis
Garrett Morgan
Mary McLeod Bethune

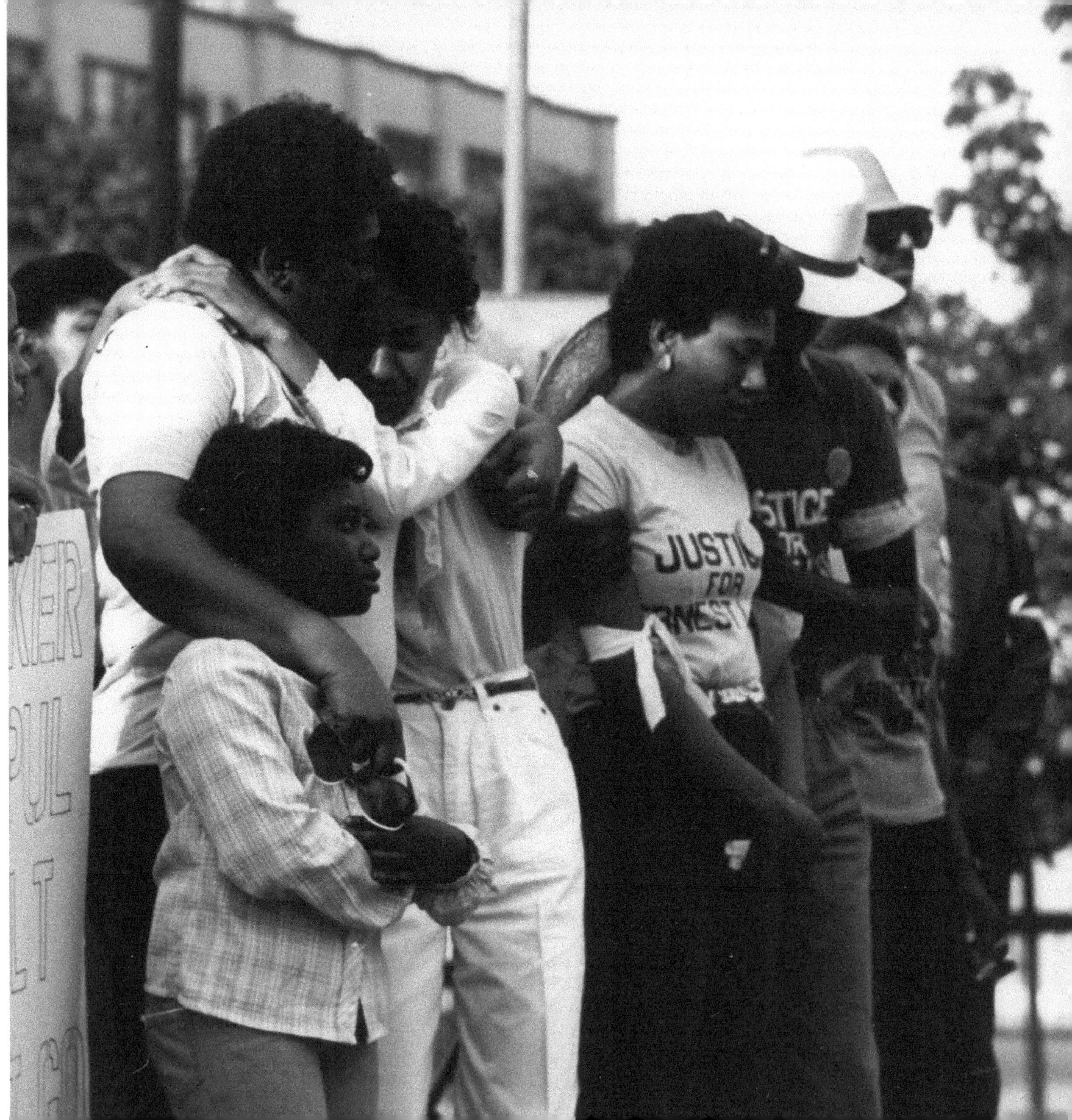
JUSTICE
FOR
RNEST
JUSTICE
FOR
RNEST

Ernest Lacy

On July 9, 1981, 22-year-old Ernest Lacy was killed in police custody. Lacy was stopped by three Milwaukee police officers who claimed he fit the description of a rape suspect from an incident earlier that evening.

A New York Times article from August 16, 1981, recounted the following details:

An eyewitness stated that the officers put handcuffs on Lacy behind his back. As two officers held down Lacy's legs, "a third officer placed his knee between Mr. Lacy's shoulder blades, forcing him to lie face down with his left cheek pinned to the ground." The officers pulled Mr. Lacy's arms up "beyond his shoulder blades and over his ears." After a violent, convulsive seizure, Lacy became lifeless and was placed in the back of a police van. An independent medical examiner later determined that "the extension of Mr. Lacy's arms toward his head interfered with the flow of oxygen to his lungs" and proved fatal.

Later identification from the rape victim confirmed that Lacy was not the suspect.

The three police officers argued they were "guilty of no wrongdoing," a claim supported by the chief of police, Harold Breier. A coroner's inquest was conducted after three autopsies yielded inconclusive findings. The jury recommended charges of homicide by reckless conduct for the three arresting officers, as well as charges of misconduct in public office for failure to render first aid and failure to inform medical personnel of Lacy's condition for one of the arresting officers and two of the officers in the police van. All of the charges were subsequently dismissed. The Fire and Police Commission later found all five officers guilty of failure to provide first aid and one of the officers guilty of excessive force. The officer found guilty of excessive force was fired; the others received suspensions.

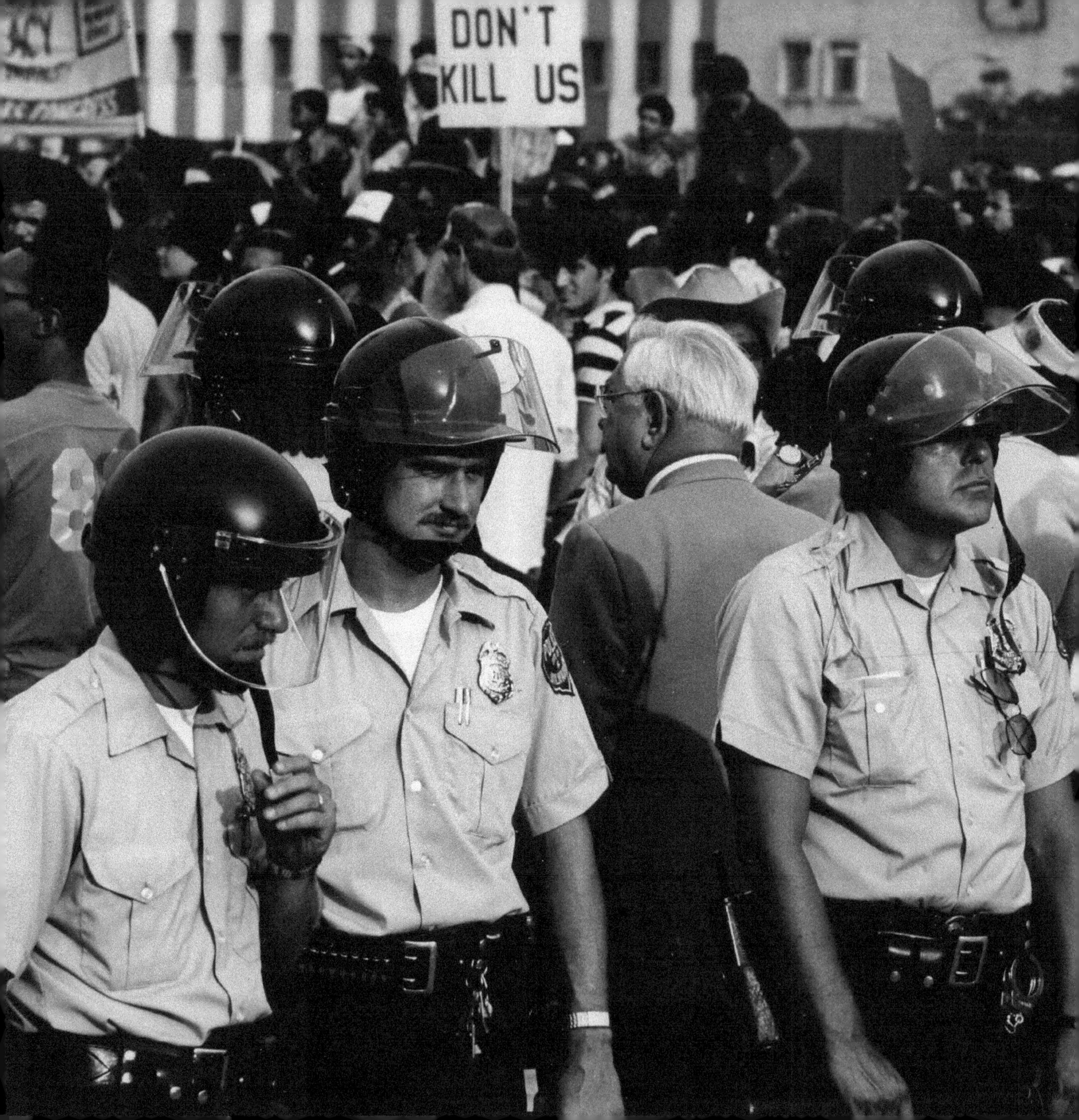
DON'T
KILL US

The Lacy family filed a suit in U.S. District Court for civil damages against the City of Milwaukee, Police Chief Harold Breier, and the five officers involved in the arrest. In September 1985, the City of Milwaukee settled the suit out of court.

In response to Lacy's death, the Wisconsin State Legislature passed statute 940.291, also known as Lacy's Law, which reads, in part, "Any police officer, while acting in the course of employment or under the authority of employment, who intentionally fails to render or make arrangements for any necessary first aid for any person in his or her actual custody is guilty of a Class A misdemeanor if bodily harm results from the failure."

In his pamphlet An Open Letter . . . Regarding the Ernest Lacy Complaint, Dr. James Cameron, founder of America's Black Holocaust Museum, writes: "Milwaukee has had her share of a carnival of police brutality blood, as gory as can be found anywhere."

Retired circuit court judge Robert C. Cannon (left) presides over the Ernest Lacy inquest in 1981, acting as a special medical examiner. Under pressure from the Coalition for Justice for Ernest Lacy, the regular examiner disqualified himself after telling a reporter he did not think a jury could find enough evidence to charge any of the officers.

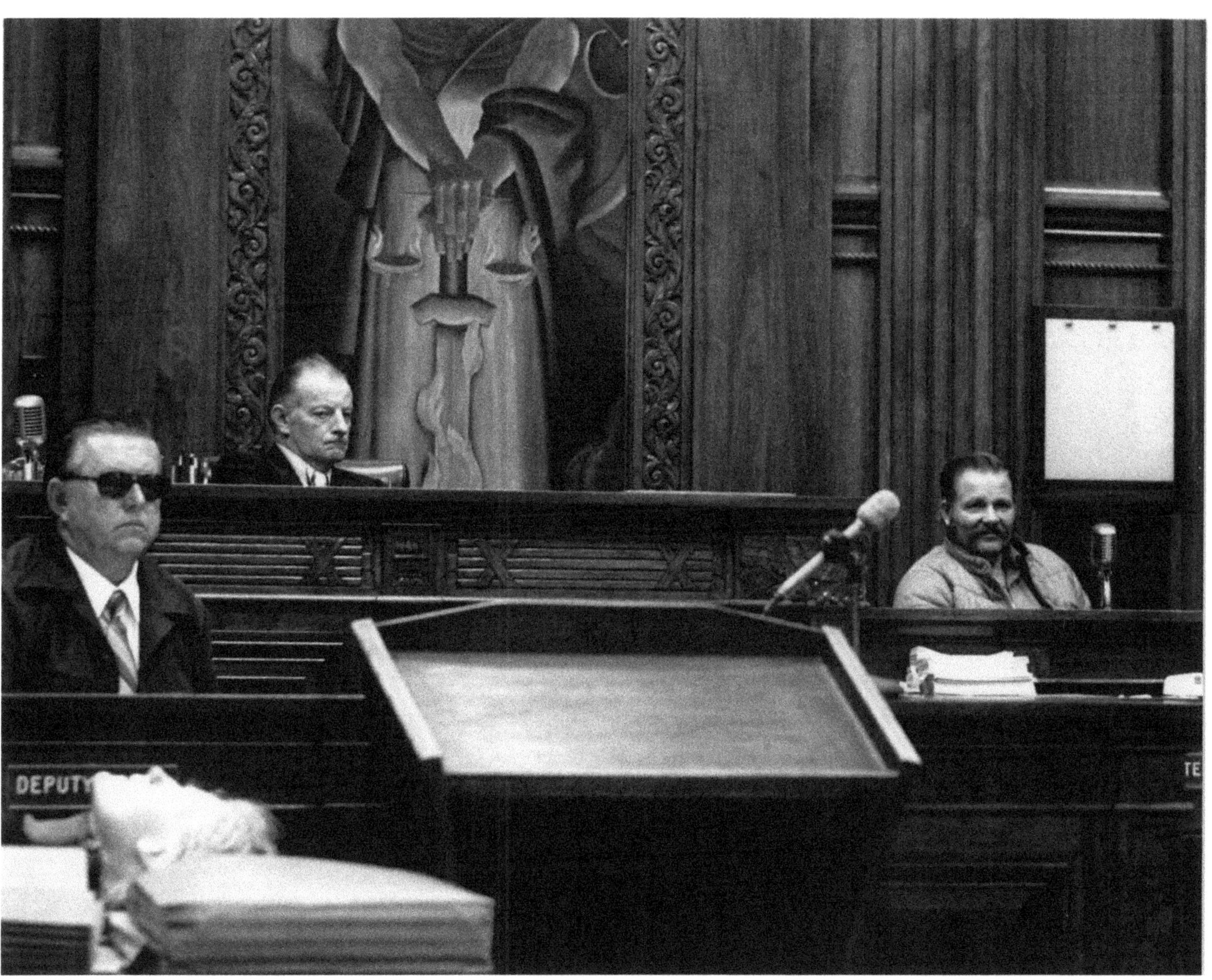

DEPUTY

Ernest Lacy March and Rally—7/9/1982

On the one-year anniversary of Ernest Lacy's murder, several hundred demonstrators marched from 23rd Street and Wisconsin Avenue, the place of Lacy's death, to the downtown Civic Center Plaza. In direct response, 110 Milwaukee police officers were ordered by Police Chief Harold Breier to line the streets.

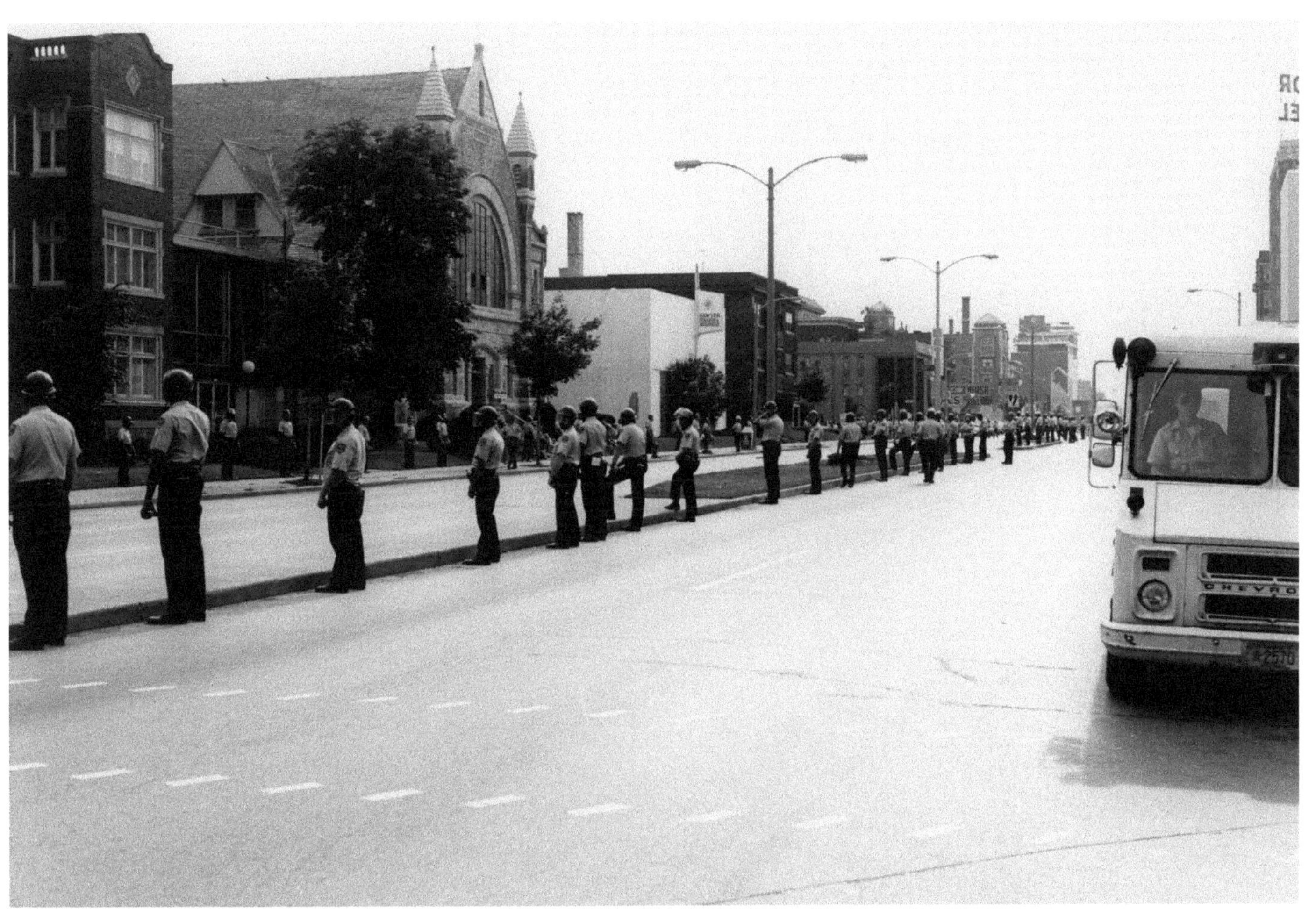

Ernest Lacy March and Rally—7/9/1982

During the July 9, 1982, Ernest Lacy march and rally, Police Chief Harold Breier (center with his back toward the camera) and Milwaukee police officers surrounded the protesters in front of the Milwaukee County Service Center / State Office Building in MacArthur Square.

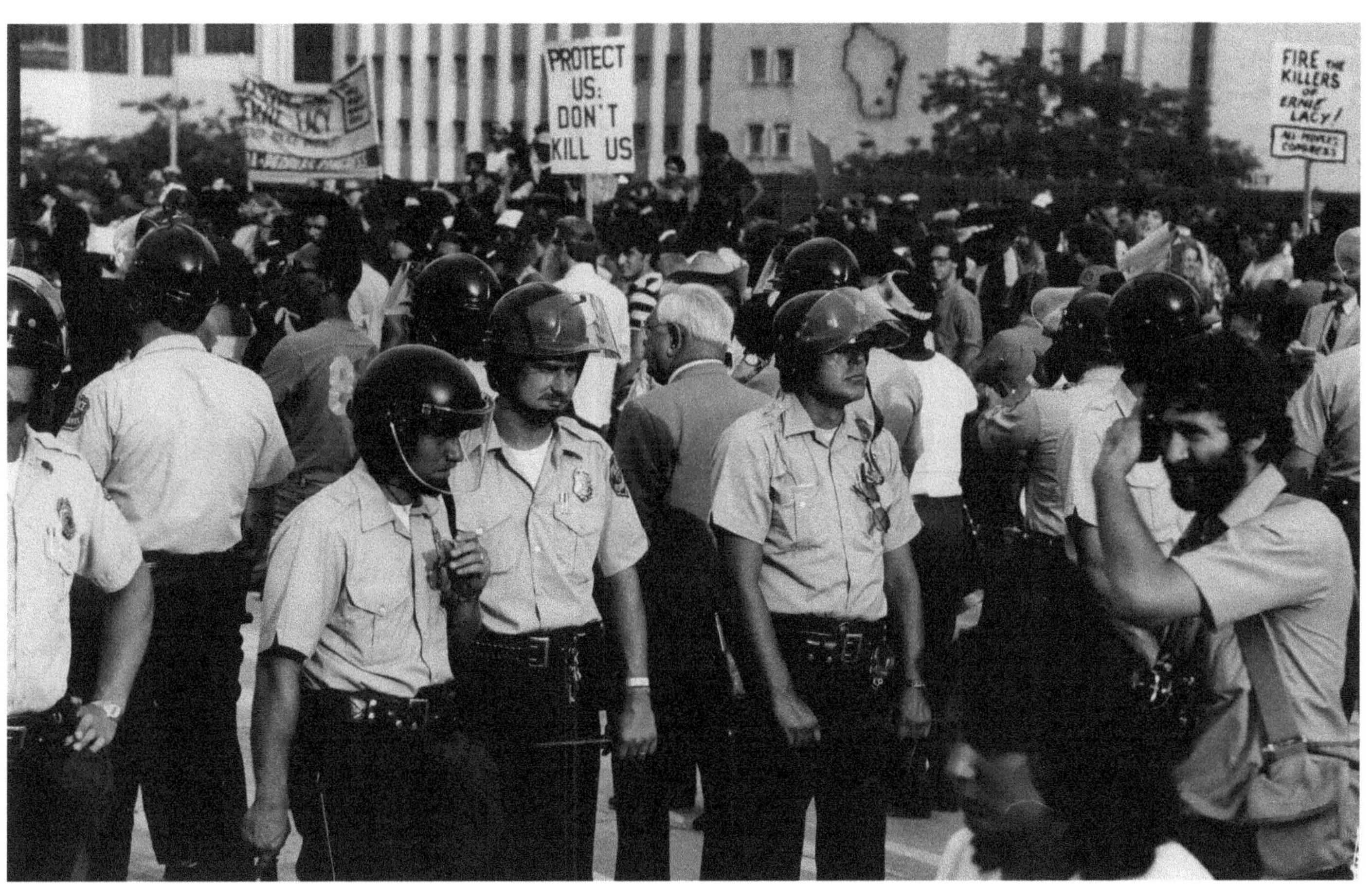
PROTECT
US:
DON'T
KILL US
FIRE THE
KILLERS
OF
ERNIE
LACY!

Ernest Lacy March and Rally—7/9/1982

On the one-year anniversary of the murder of Ernest Lacy, protestors representing numerous groups demonstrated in demand for justice.

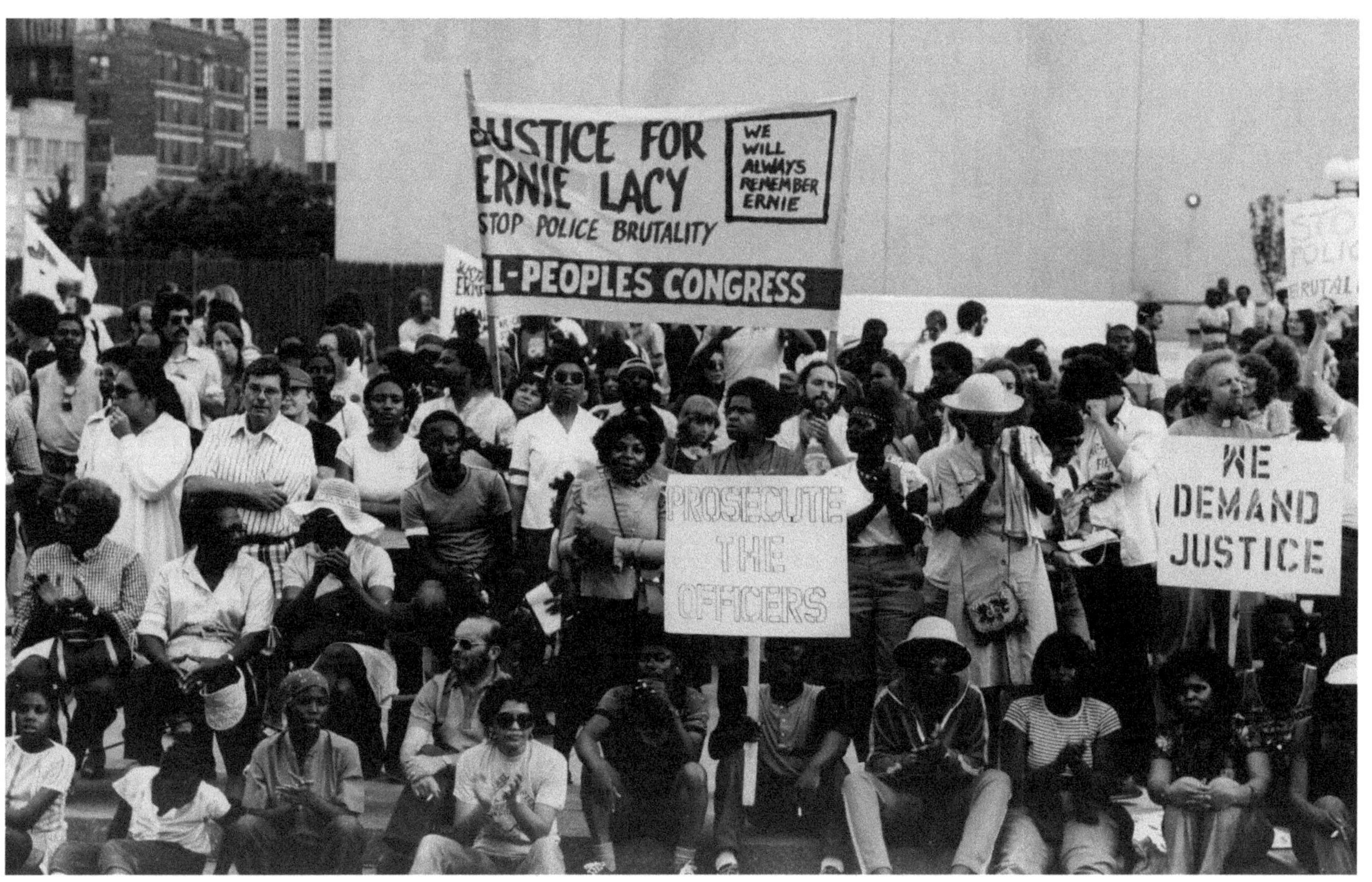
JUSTICE FOR
ERNIE LACY
STOP POLICE BRUTALITY
WE WILL ALWAYS REMEMBER ERNIE
L-PEOPLES CONGRESS
PROSECUTE THE OFFICERS
WE DEMAND JUSTICE
STOP POLICE BRUTALITY

Ernest Lacy March and Rally—7/9/1982
Print from digital scan

A year after the murder of Ernest Lacy, marchers protest the dismissal of charges against the officers directly involved in his death—George Kalt, James Dekker, and Thomas Eliopul. One sign reads, "Justice Delayed Is Justice Denied," a saying referring to the right for a speedy trial and a phrase used by Martin Luther King Jr. in his Letter from Birmingham Jail.

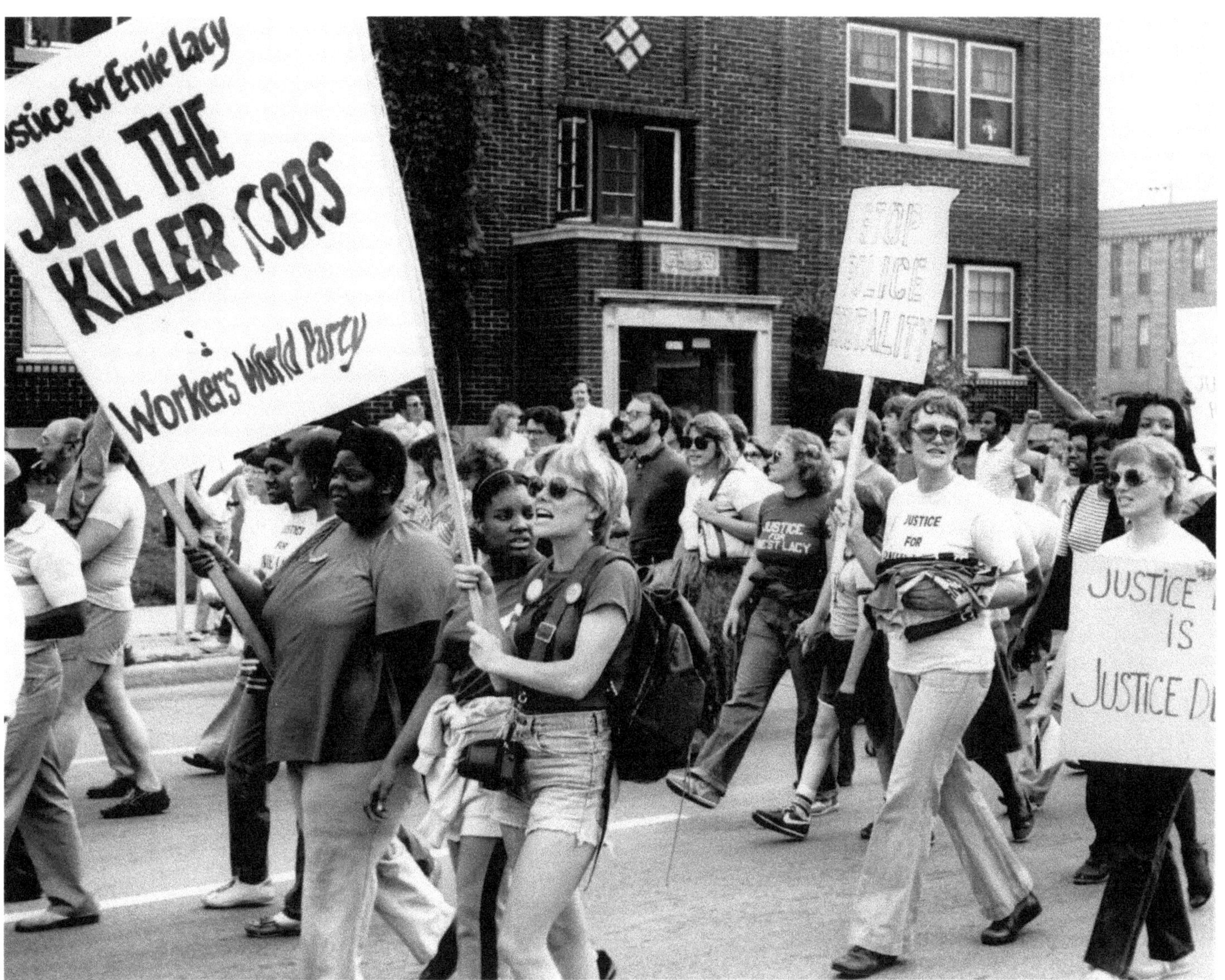
Justice for Ernie Lacy
JAIL THE KILLER COPS
Workers World Party
STOP POLICE BRUTALITY
JUSTICE FOR ERNIE LACY
JUSTICE IS JUSTICE D

Ernest Lacy March and Rally—7/9/1982

A year after the murder of Ernest Lacy, his family continued to seek justice in the charging of the officers responsible for his death. Participants in the July 1982 march and rally embrace and bow their heads in mourning.

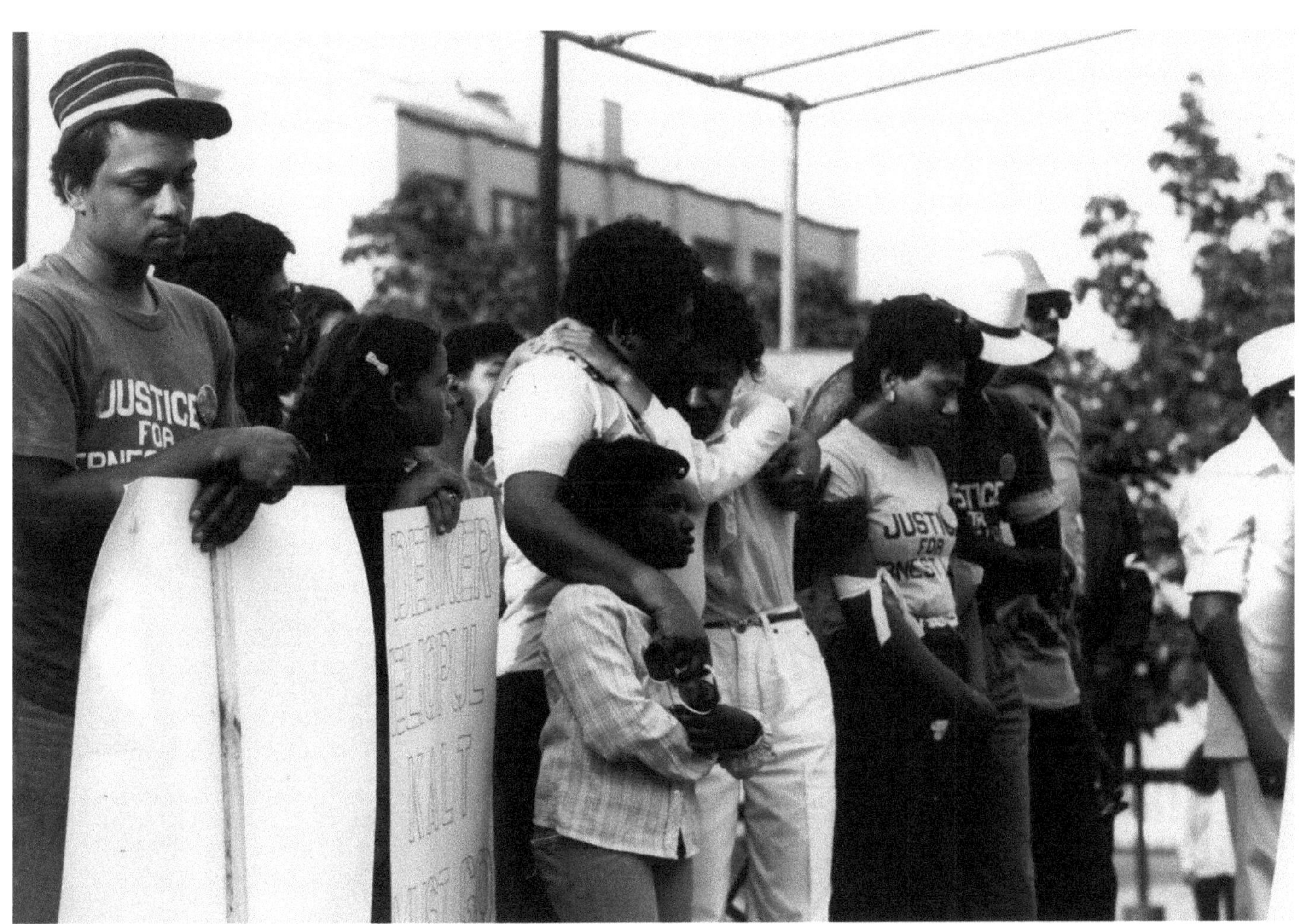

Lacy Family at Lacy Rally at Incarnation Lutheran Church, 1983

Myrtle and Leonardo Lacy (mother and father of Ernest Lacy) seated at the altar of Incarnation Lutheran Church on Keefe Avenue and 15th Street on April 7, 1983. They are accompanied by members of the Coalition for Justice for Ernest Lacy, Hubert C. Canfield and future Milwaukee Alderman Michael McGee Jr.

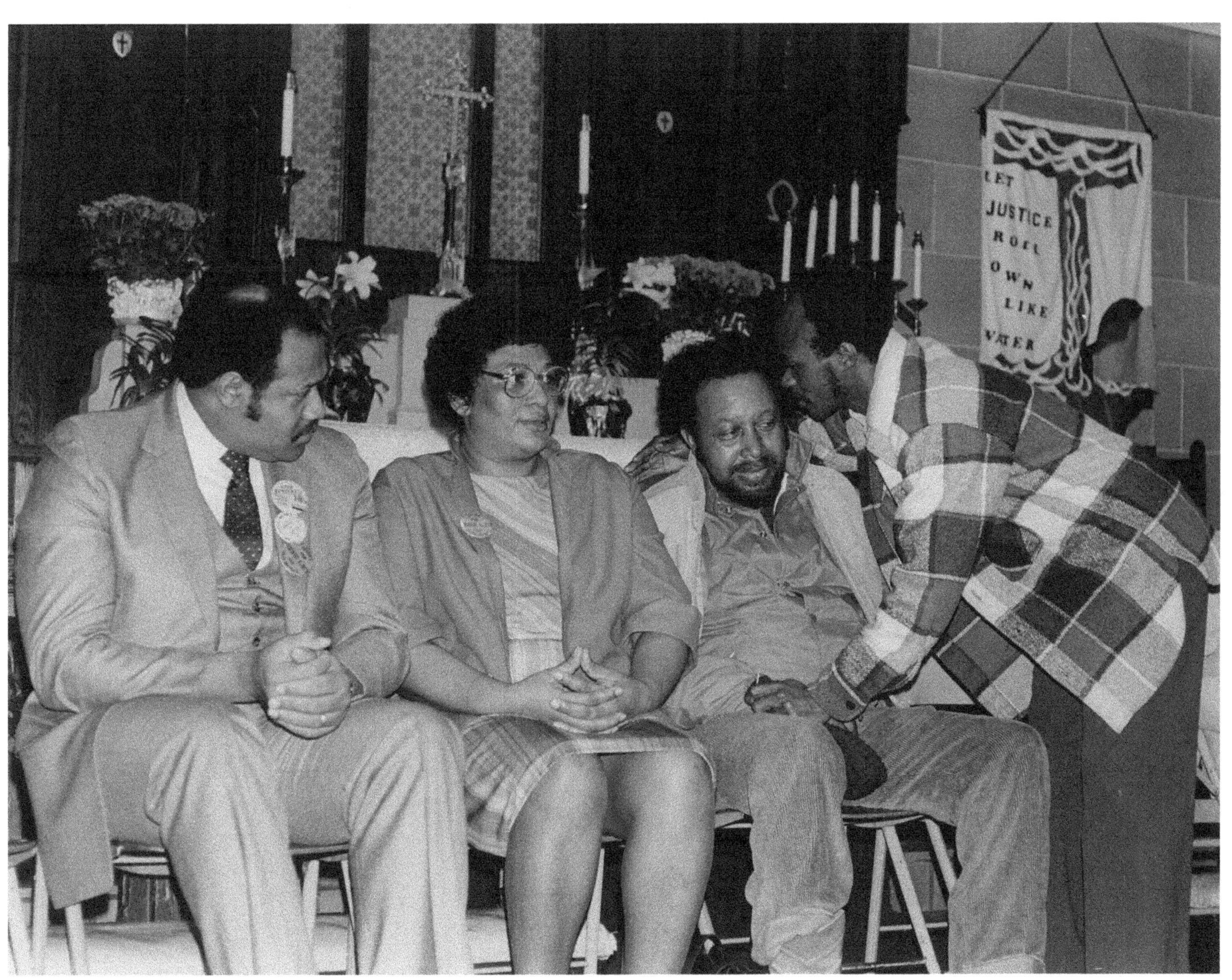
LET
JUSTICE
ROLL
DOWN
LIKE
WATER

Myrtle Lacy—5/20/1983

Two years after the death of Ernest Lacy, his mother, Myrtle, and sister Kim spoke with WISN-12 News after the Milwaukee Fire and Police Commission found five Milwaukee police officers (James Dekker, George Kalt, Robert Enters, Kenneth Kinichick, and Thomas Eliopul) guilty of failing to render first aid to Lacy while in custody. Officer Eliopul was also found guilty of using excessive force in the arrest.

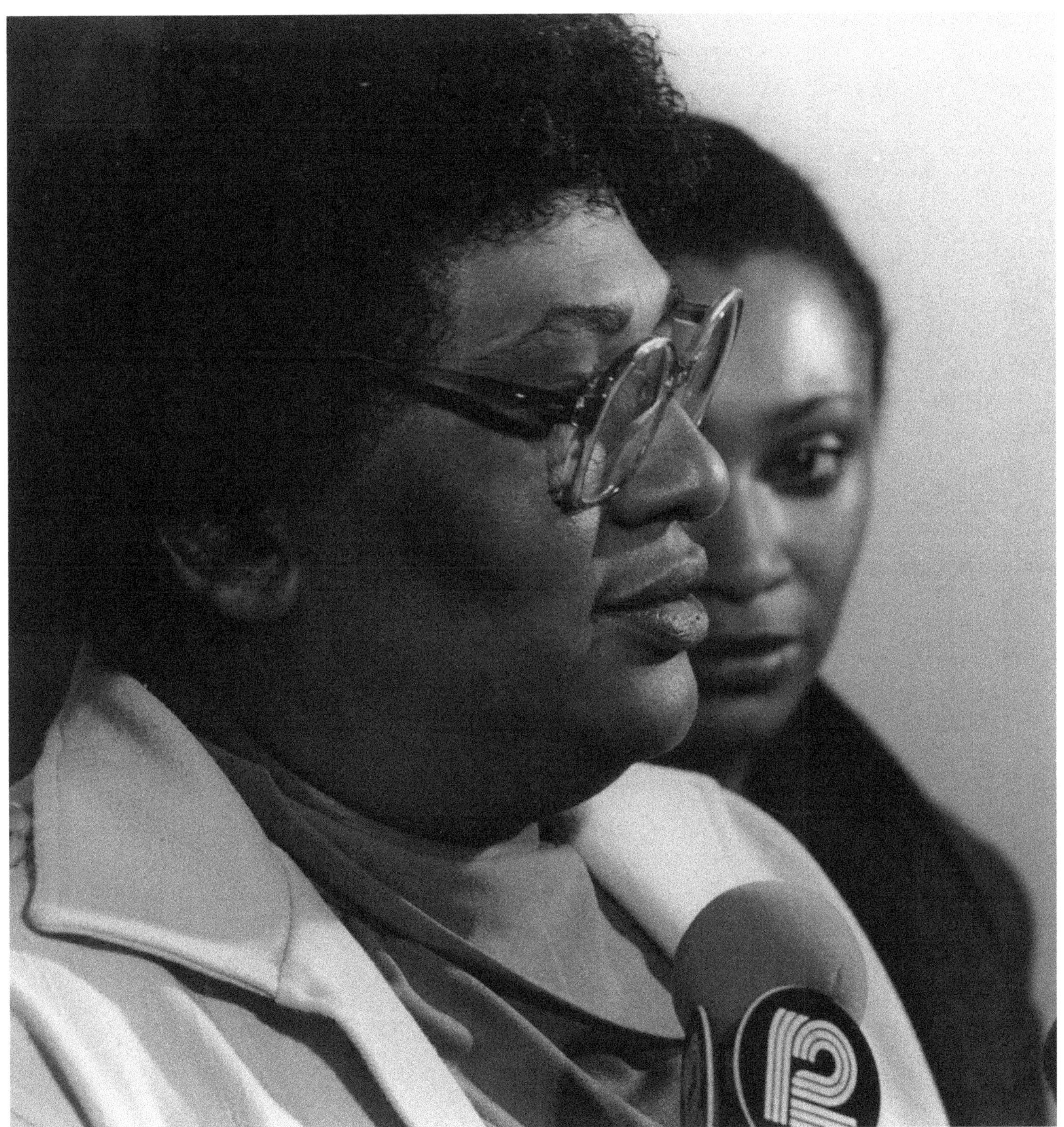

MILWAUKEE

COMMUNITY JOURNAL

3612 NORTH GREEN BAY AVENUE

MILWAUKEE, WISCONSIN 53212

(414) 265-5300

From the Desk of...

Michael Holt, Editor

October 19, 1981

Bill
this is a copy
of the letter sent out
Wednesday; to McCann
& others

The Honorable Robert Cannon
700 North Water Street
Milwaukee

Dear Sir:

This letter is to express our concern over the manner in which one of
our free lance photographers was treated during the recent Ernest Lacy
Inquest. Despite credentials, photographer Bill Tennessen was on
three occasions ejected from your courtroom. In addition to the
obvious embarrassment to Mr. Tennessen, your actions also resulted in
our losing the opportunity to secure a very important photograph of a
key witness in the proceedings.

To refresh your memory sir, on the occasion of Mr. Tennessen's first
attempt to secure photographs he was told he could not do so until a
letter varifying his status with our publication was received by you.
Two days later, Mr. Tennessen was again ejected from the courtroom.
When I attempted to find out why he was not allowed to photograph the
proceedings, I was told by a Deputy Sheriff that you were concerned a-
bout the possibility of his working for more than one publication. After
assurances from me that such was not the case, I was told he would again
be allowed to photograph the inquest.

Several days later Mr. Tennessen was ejected from the courtroom. At
that time Mr. Tennessen was photographing the proceedings when another
of my photographers entered the courtroom. According to Mr. Tennessen
and several witnesses, you very rudely dismissed him, citing the ap-
pearance of photographer Harry Kemp as your justification.

Your actions sir, caused considerable damage to the creditability of
Mr. Tennessen and to this publication.

As I informed you in previous correspondence, the Community Journal is
the largest circulated Black publication in the State of Wisconsin. Despite that fact, we neither have the resources nor the manpower to as-

sign either reporter or photographer, on a full time basis, to cover
the inquest. Moreover, it is my understanding that the city's white
dailies each had more than one representative at the proceeding at any
given time. This implies to me, and others who are familiar with this
situation, that the courts are once again establishing separate standards
for the white and Black press.

I sincerely hope, sir, that this is not the case and that other considera-
tions prompted your actions. We, however, have found ourselves under
similar circumstances with other branches of government in the past and
have in each case taken proper actions to correct the problem.

Your response is requested.

                         Very truly yours,

                         Michael Holt
                         Editor   MCJ

cc
District Attorney
Coalition for Justice for Ernie Lacy
Black elected officials

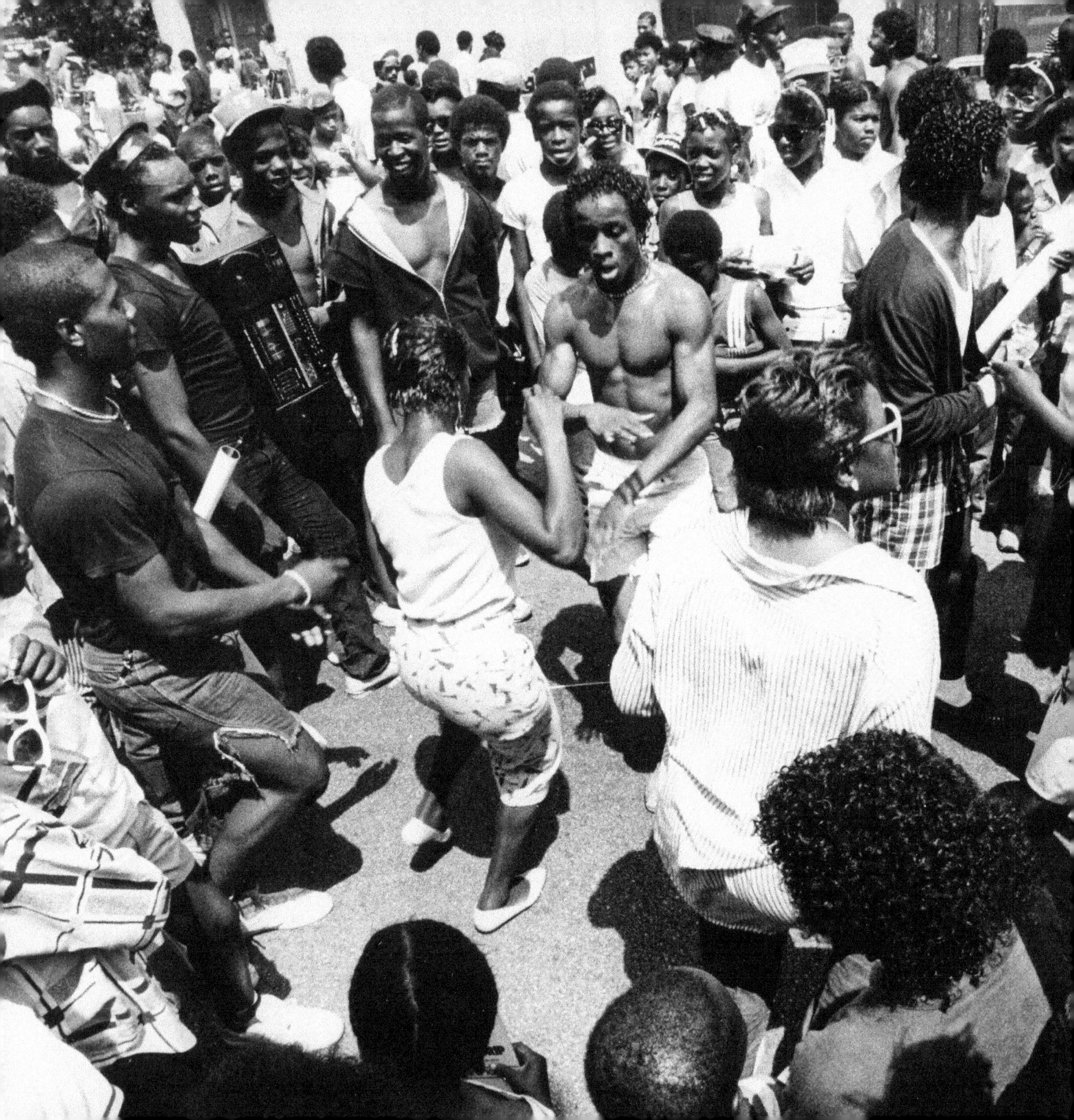

Juneteenth

As the oldest nationally celebrated commemoration of the ending of slavery in the United States, Juneteenth is arguably the most important holiday in this country. On June 19, 1865, enslaved African Americans in the westernmost part of the Confederacy (Galveston, Texas) were informed of the ending of slavery. While not technically the date of slavery's end, Juneteenth (a combination of June and nineteenth) was adopted as the day to celebrate freedom.

Milwaukee has one of the largest and longest-running Juneteenth celebrations outside of the South. This year marks 53 years of recognizing Juneteenth in the city. Juneteenth Day 2024 will also mark the 36th anniversary of the founding of America's Black Holocaust Museum.

With these photographs, Tennessen preserves and shares the joy and communal love that characterize these celebrations. The photos also reveal how these celebrations of freedom are intergenerational, connecting America with the larger African diaspora, and connecting contemporary experiences to the Black past in the United States.

Juneteenth Day Celebration, 1983

Juneteenth Day festivities in 1983 on the historic stretch of Dr. Martin Luther King Jr. Drive (formerly North Third Street) between Burleigh and Center Streets. This part of MLK Drive has closed every year for the event since the first Juneteenth Day celebration in 1971.

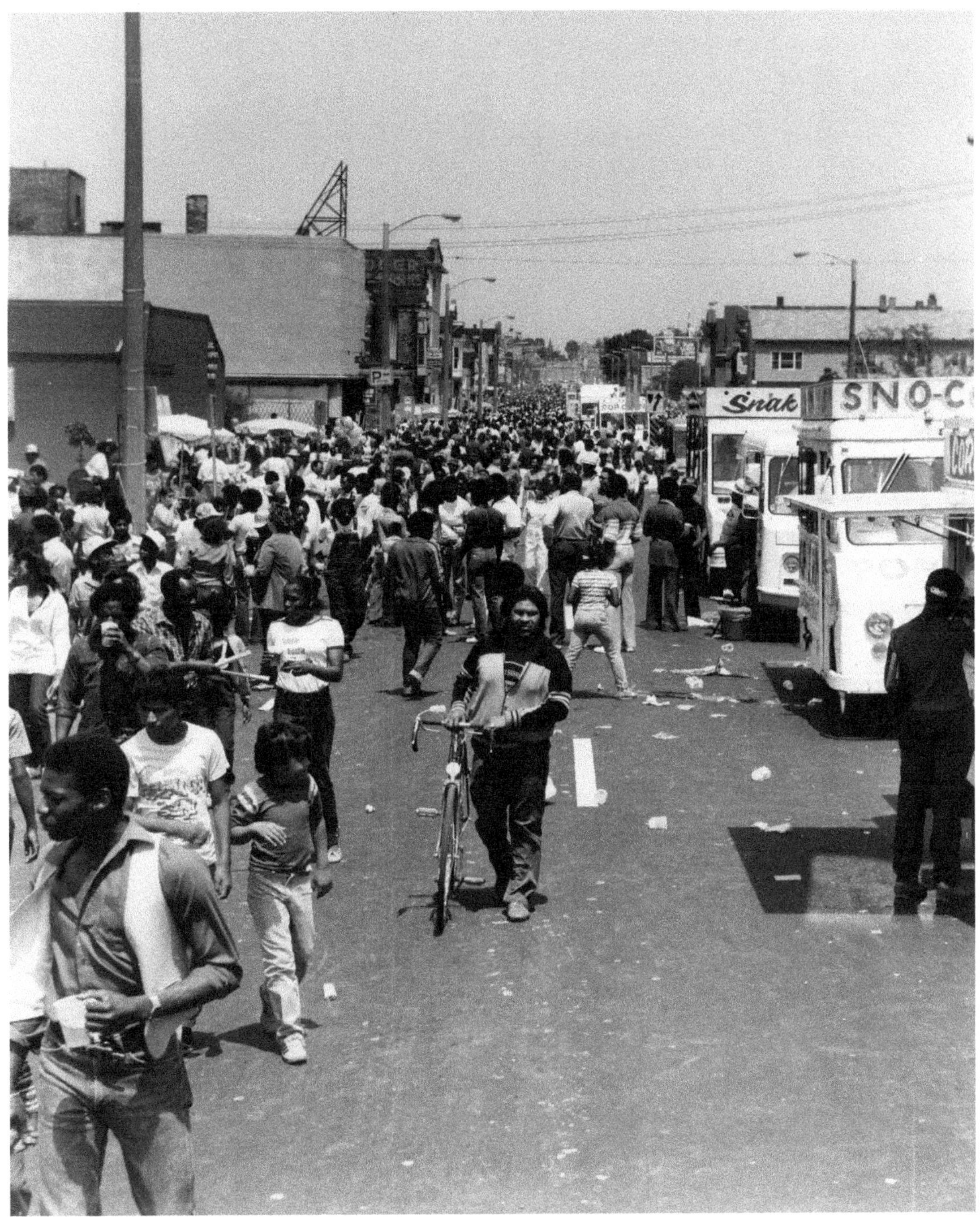

Juneteenth Day Celebration, 1985

Milwaukee youth celebrate Juneteenth Day in 1985. Hip hop's aesthetics and Afro-Caribbean polyrhythms became central to Juneteenth Day celebrations, with Milwaukee youth driving the culture locally.

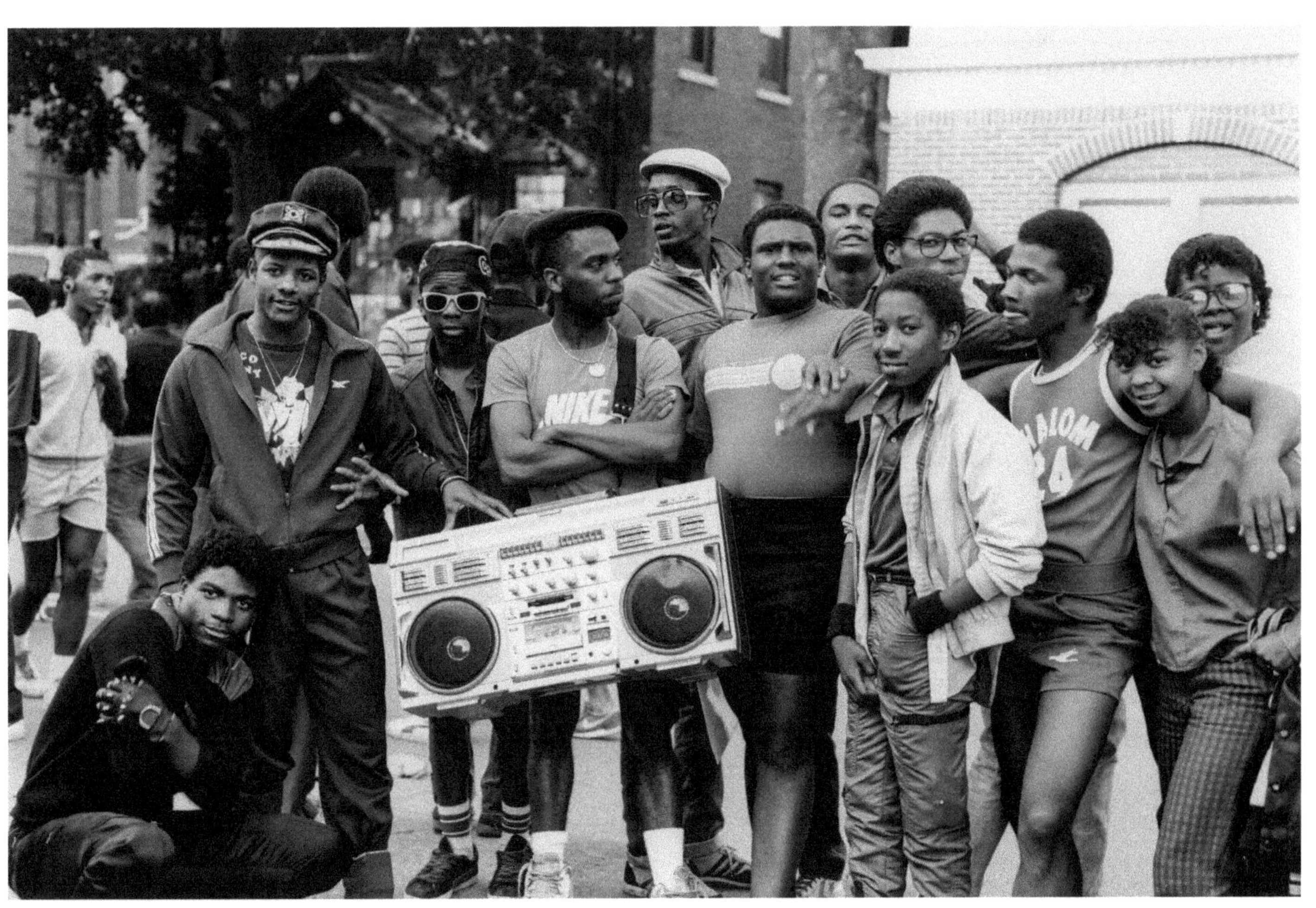

Juneteenth Day Celebration, 1986

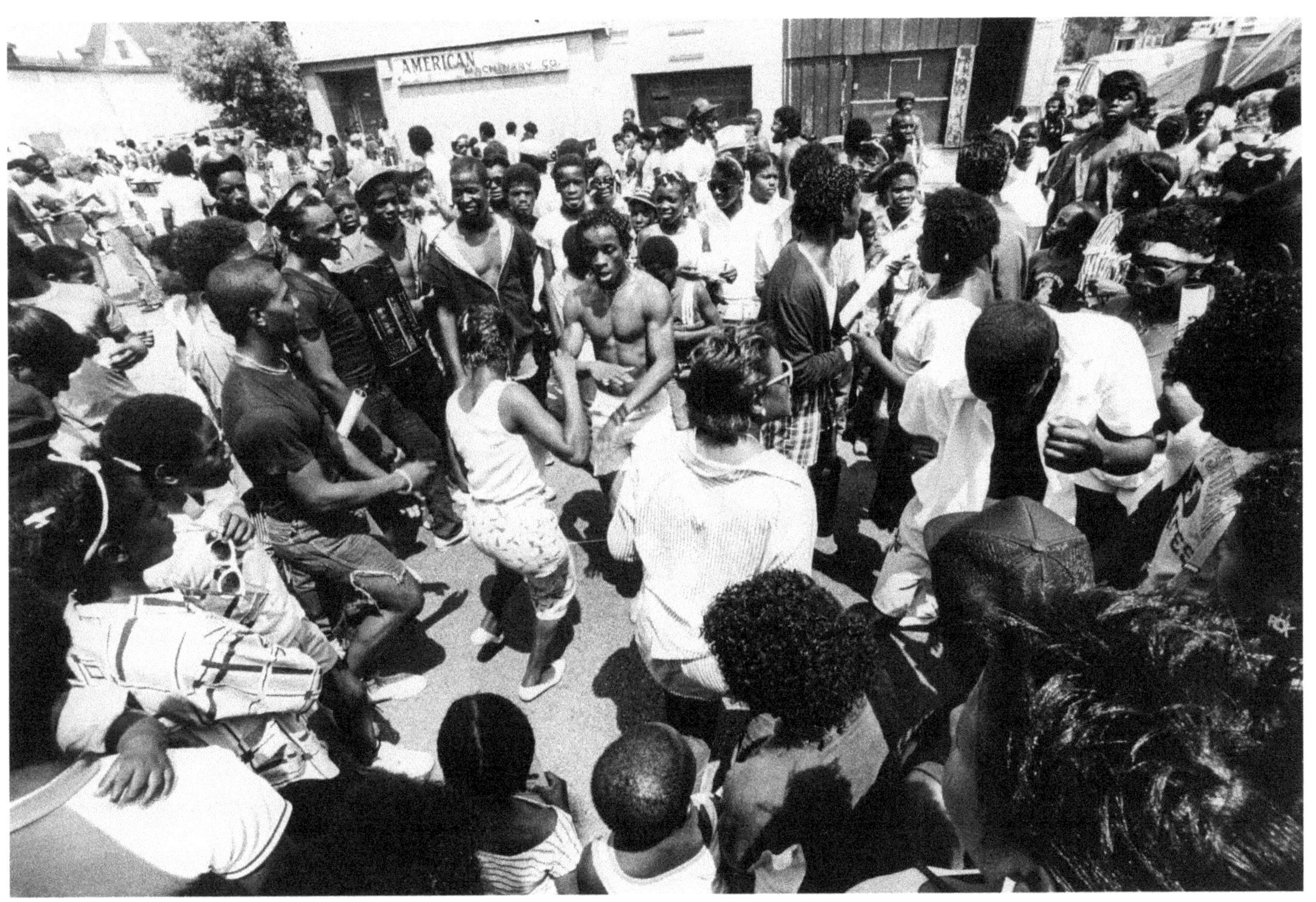
AMERICAN
MACHINERY CO.

Juneteenth Day Celebration, 1990

Members of Oyotunji Yoruba African Kingdom visit Milwaukee for Juneteenth Day celebrations. Now known as the Oyotunji African Village (OAV), this South Carolina based communal group was the first organization in the Americas rooted in the Yoruba and Dahomey cultures of West Africa. The group partnered with Ko-Thi Dance Company to provide entertainment for the festivities.

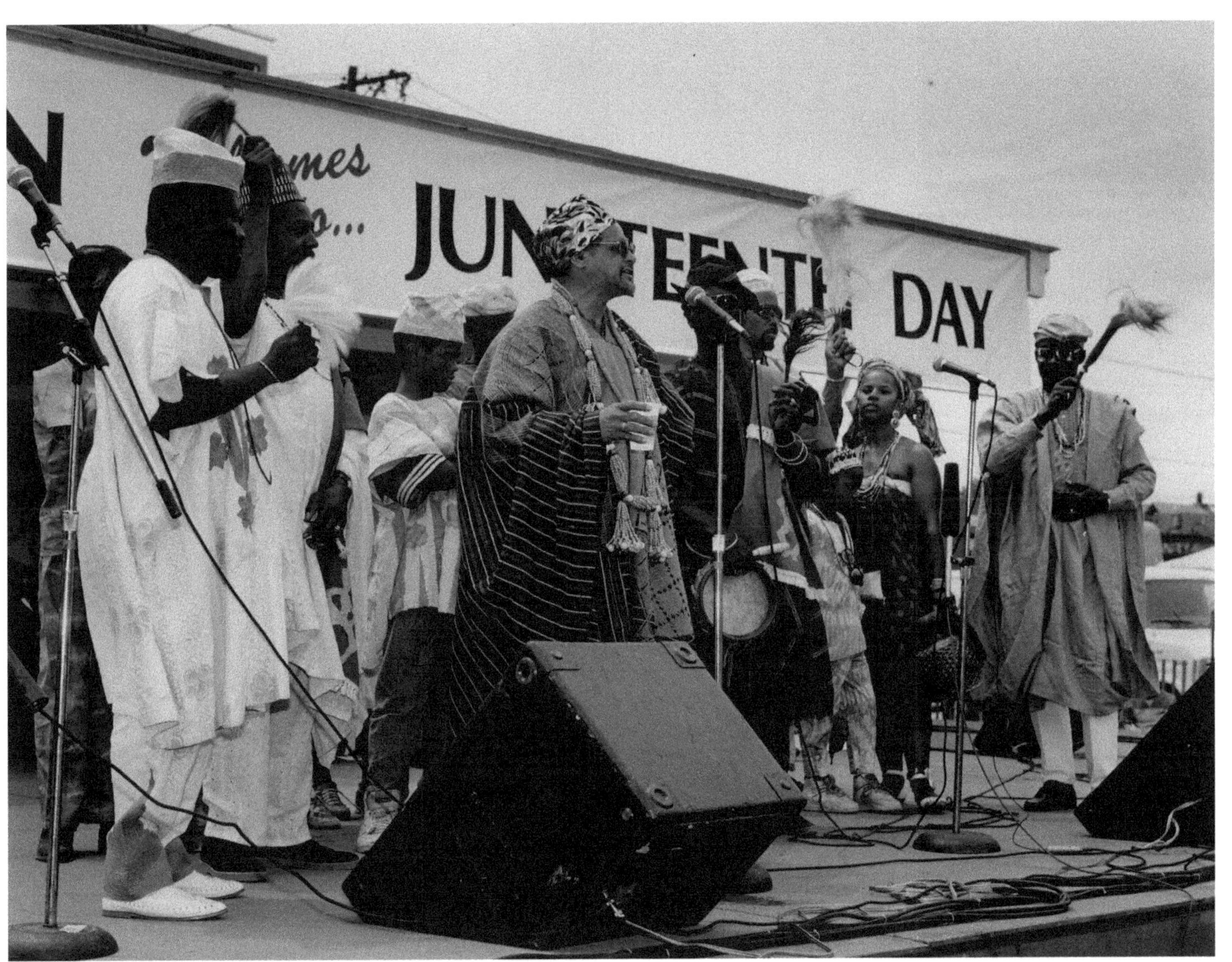
JUNETEENTH DAY

Juneteenth Day Celebration, 1991

Pictured here is a rider from the Wisconsin Black Cowboys and Buffalo Soldiers Association at the Juneteenth Day celebration in 1991. As a national organization, the Black Cowboys Association was brought to Milwaukee during the 1970s by Isaac Steele. The Cowboys still ride their horses during the Juneteenth Day parades today. Their mission is to instill values of justice, hard work, leadership skills, and personal responsibility in Milwaukee's youth.

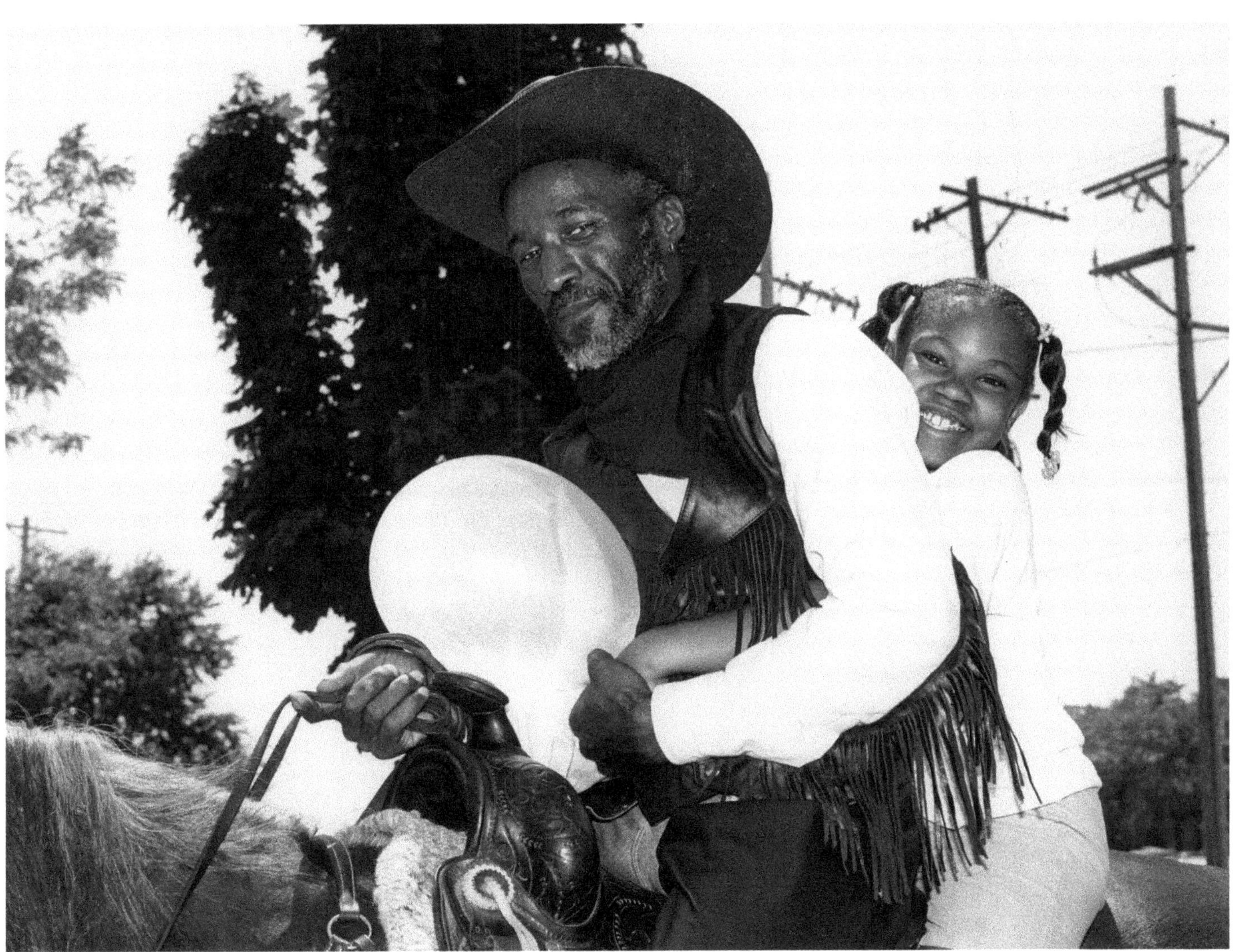

Juneteenth Day Celebration, 1989

A group of Juneteenth Day celebrators pose for a picture to honor the legacy of Black struggle in the United States. Several of the men wear shirts that display the date of June 19, 1989, along with an image of Dr. Martin Luther King Jr. and the motto "Pulling together to fulfill the dream."

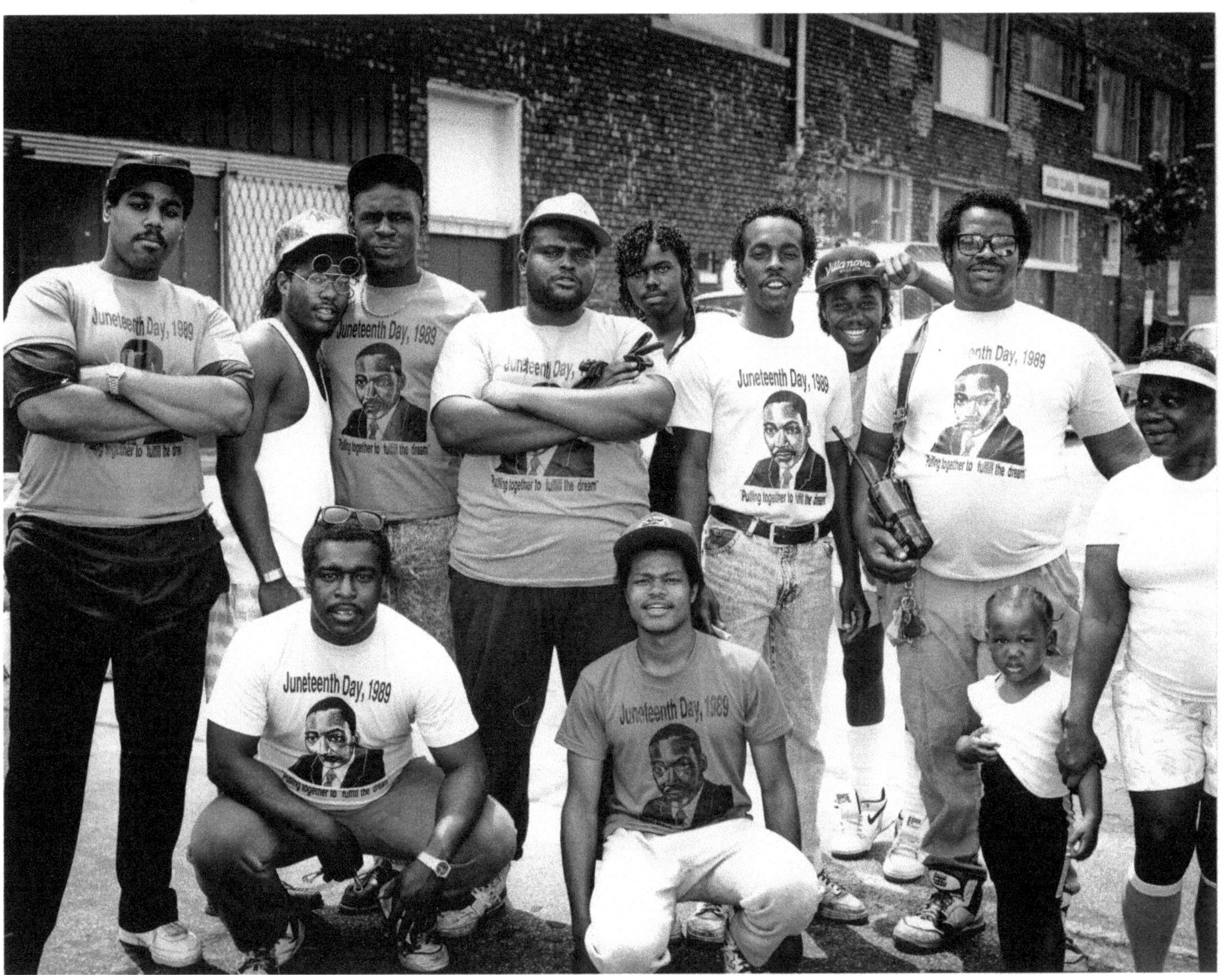

Juneteenth Day Celebration, 1985

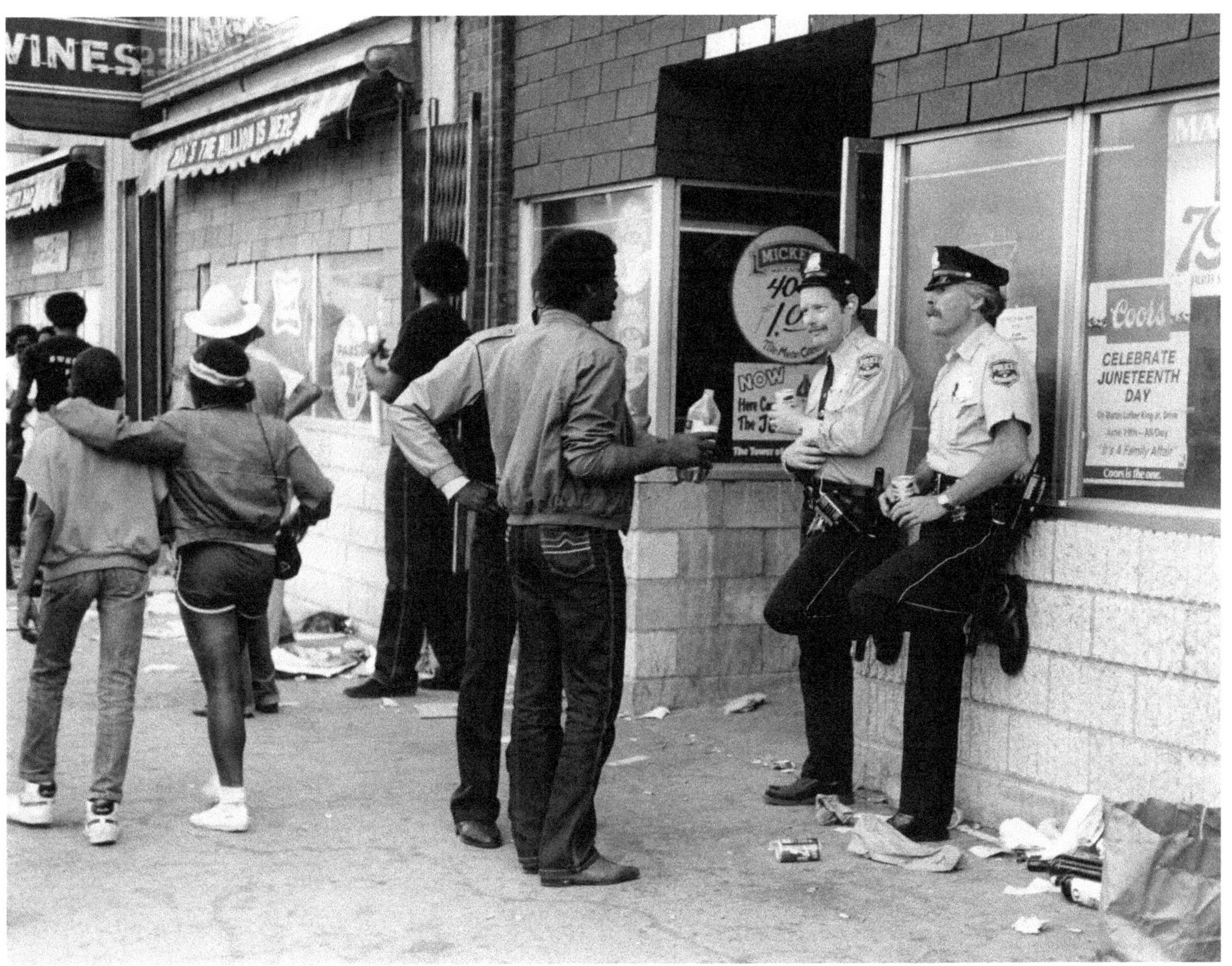
WINES
WHERE THE MILLION IS HERE
MICKEY'S
40
1.0
NOW
Here Co
The J
Coors
CELEBRATE
JUNETEENTH
DAY
It's A Family Affair
Coors is the one.
79

Juneteenth Day Celebration, 1985

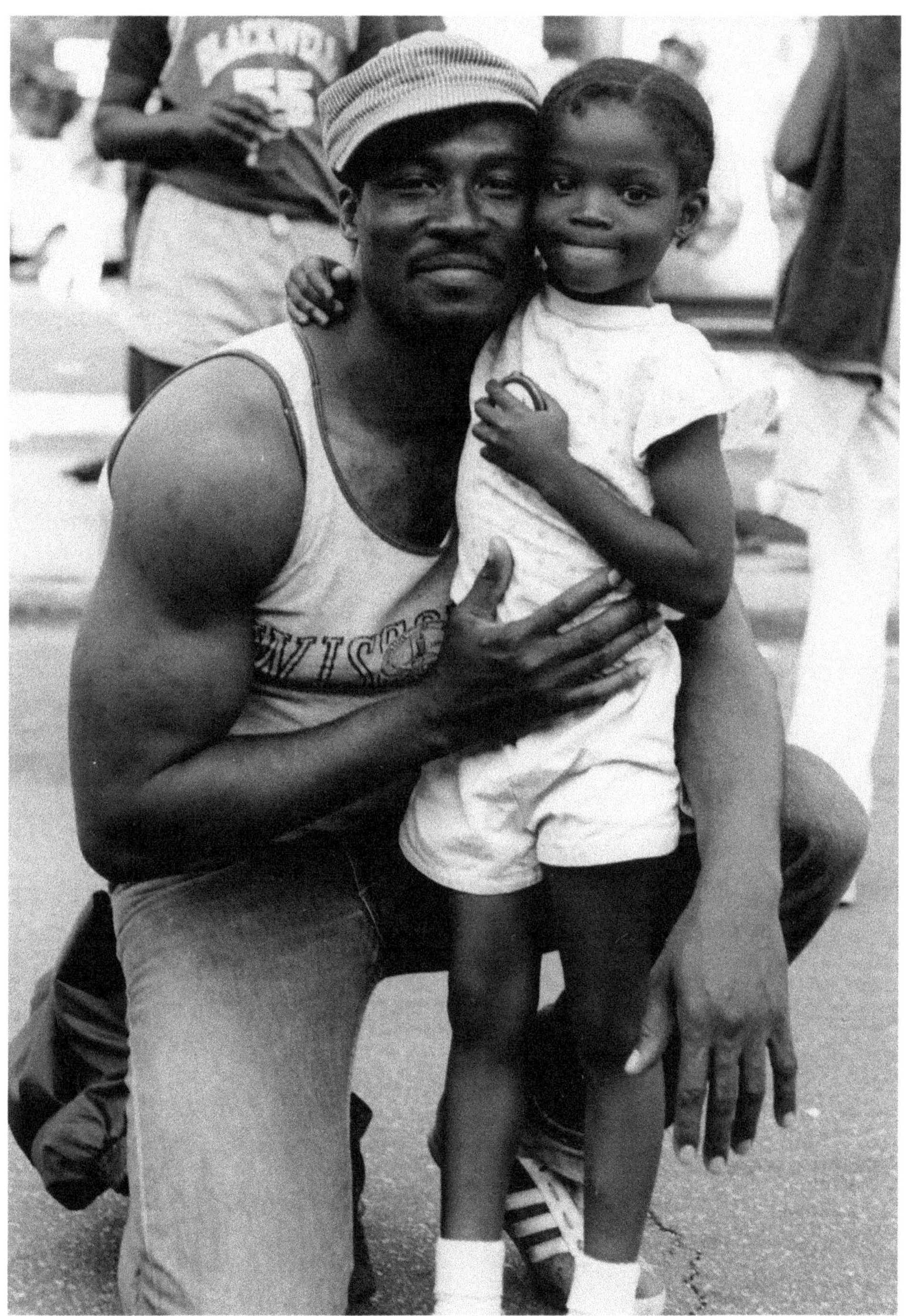

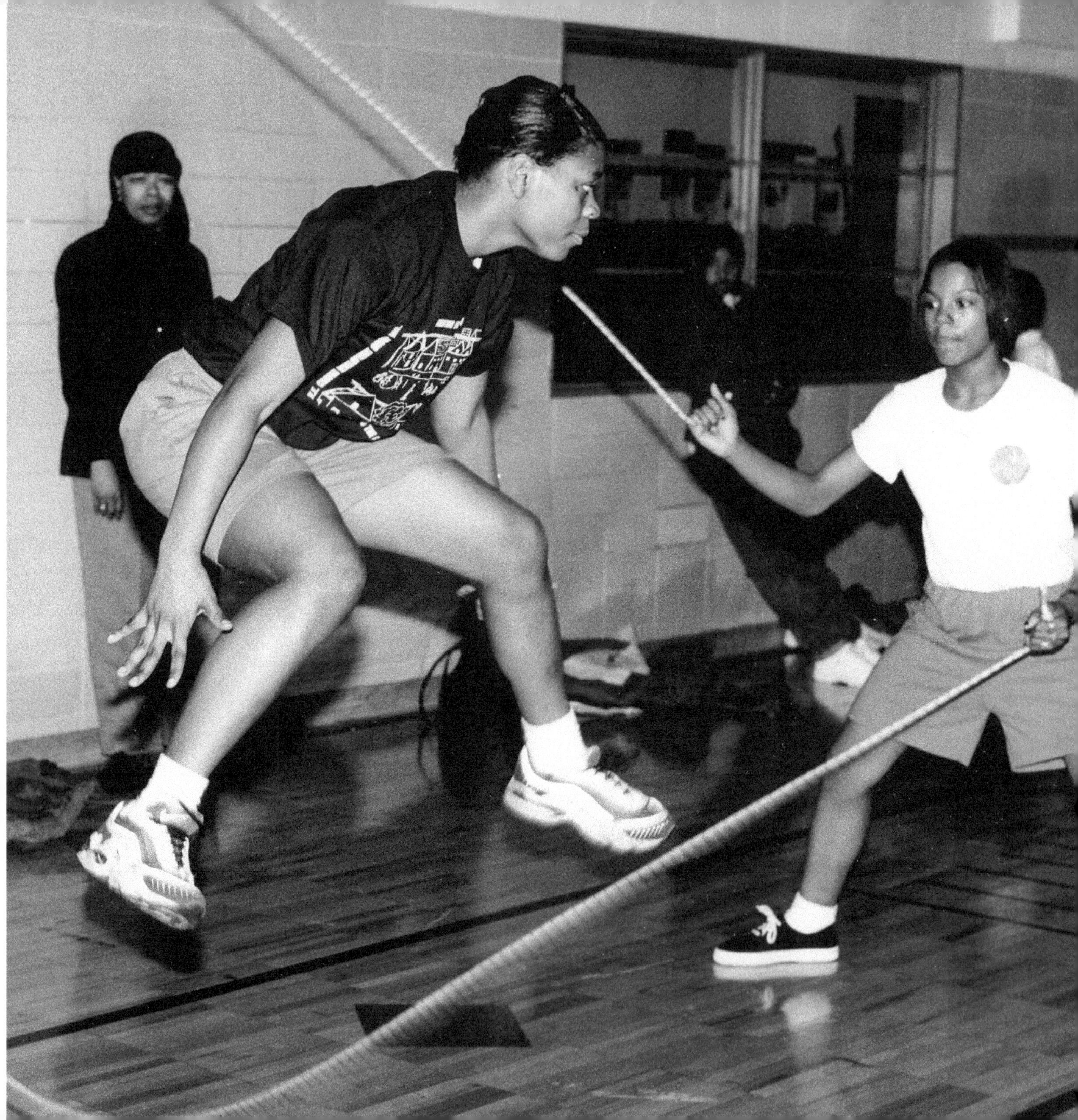

Boys & Girls Clubs of Greater Milwaukee

Supporting local children and teenagers since 1887, the Boys & Girls Clubs of Greater Milwaukee (BGCGM) is the largest youth-serving agency in the city and has grown to become one of the largest in the country. With programs that span sports, education, college access, career development, health and wellness, and leadership and social emotional development, BGCGM has a longstanding commitment to addressing some of the most pressing issues facing Milwaukee's youth.

Tennessen's photography helped ensure that the Milwaukee Community Journal consistently documented the great programs sponsored by BGCGM. Some media outlets and politicians portrayed Black youth as dangerous, undriven, and without hope, reinforcing stereotypes that persist to this day. In contrast, Tennessen's photos show the creativity, talent, and joy of Milwaukee's young Black people, as well as the ongoing investment in their livelihoods by the Boys & Girls Clubs of Greater Milwaukee.

Children's Fest was an annual event held at the Summerfest grounds as a collaboration between Summerfest and the Milwaukee Public Schools Department of Recreation. It was a free event for children held each year in late July. Similar events had taken place since 1971, but the celebration officially became Children's Fest in 1984 after Elizabeth "Bo" Black became the executive director of Summerfest.

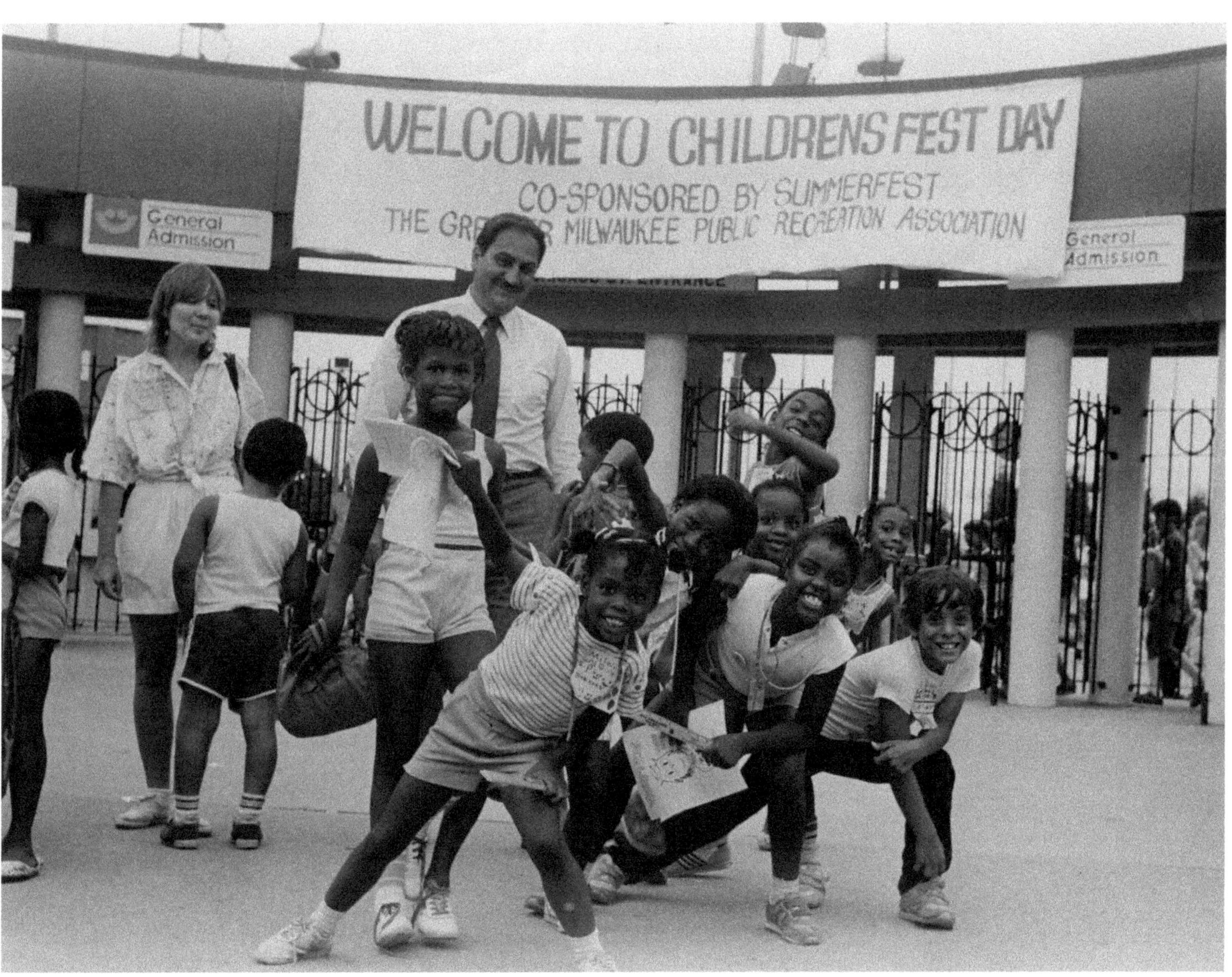

WELCOME TO CHILDRENS FEST DAY
CO-SPONSORED BY SUMMERFEST
THE GREATER MILWAUKEE PUBLIC RECREATION ASSOCIATION
General Admission
General Admission

Boys & Girls Clubs of Greater Milwaukee Sign Language Choir, 1987

On August 6, 1987, the Boys & Girls Clubs of Greater Milwaukee held Youth Health Kicks Festival in Sherman Park. This photograph shows the Boys & Girls Clubs Sign Language Choir using sign language to sing a song at the festival.

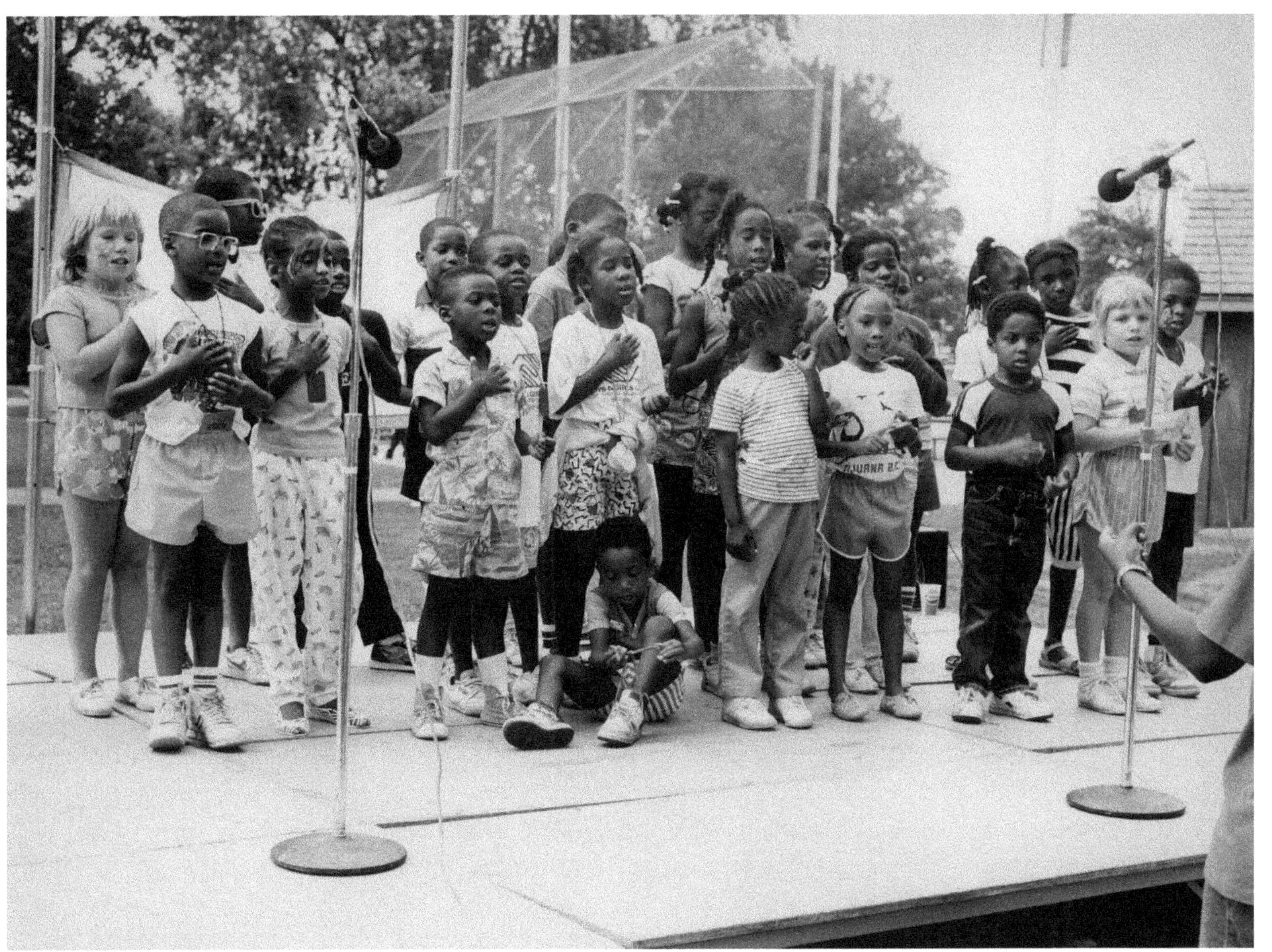

Boys & Girls Clubs of Greater Milwaukee Art Show at the Bradley Center, 1992

In 1992, the Boys & Girls Clubs of Greater Milwaukee held an art show for their members at the Bradley Center, a downtown venue that presented sporting events, concerts, etc. before it was demolished in 2019. Approximately 370 artists aged 6 to 18 participated, and over 500 works were displayed.

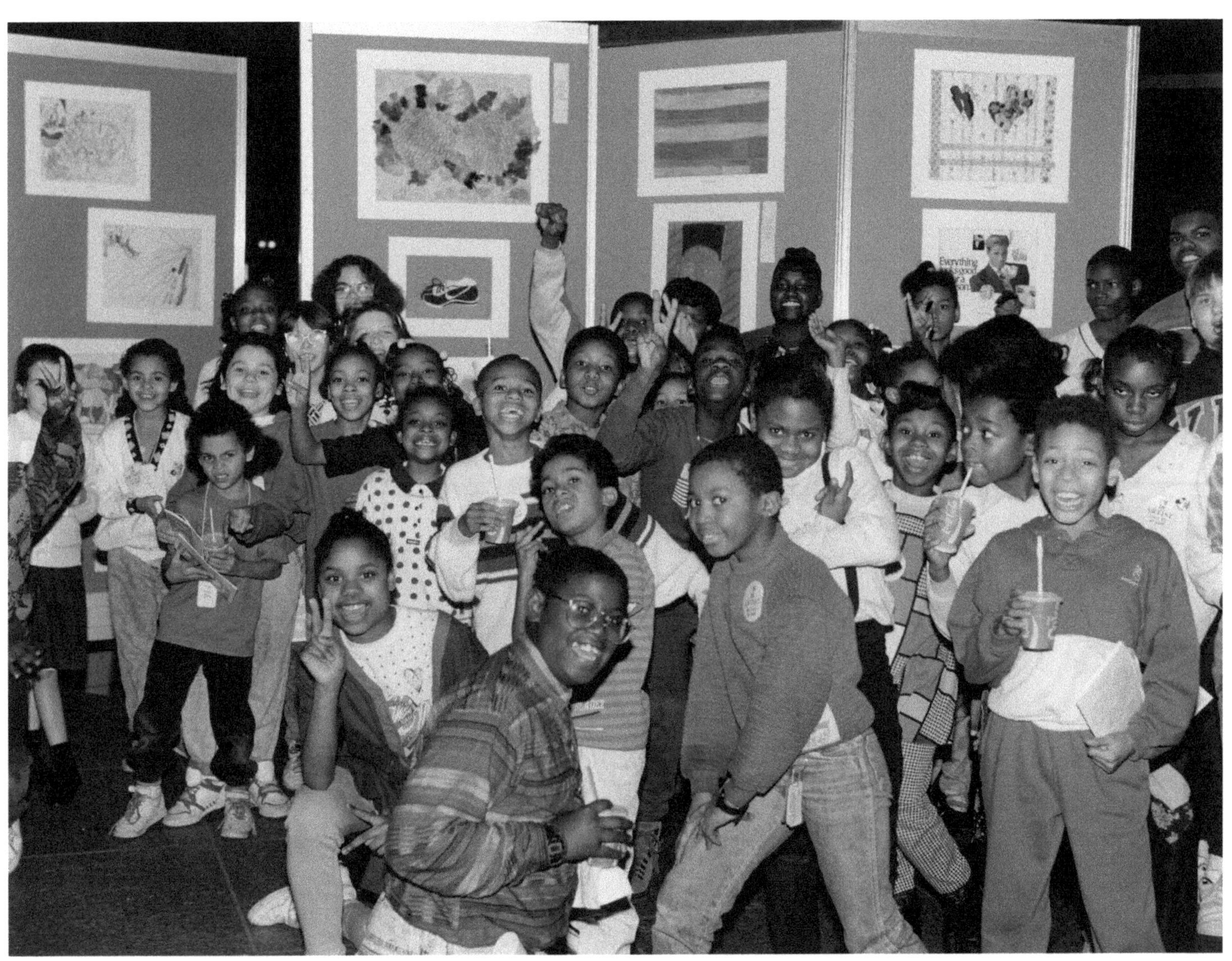

*Boys & Girls Clubs of Greater Milwaukee Members
with Gordon Parks, 1998*

Members of the Seher Boys & Girls Club meet with photographer Gordon Parks at a Milwaukee Art Museum event in 1998. Gordon Parks was known for his photographs and films that document African American life and history. Exploring themes of poverty, urban living, history, and race relations, Parks's work has been instrumental in raising awareness of racial inequity.

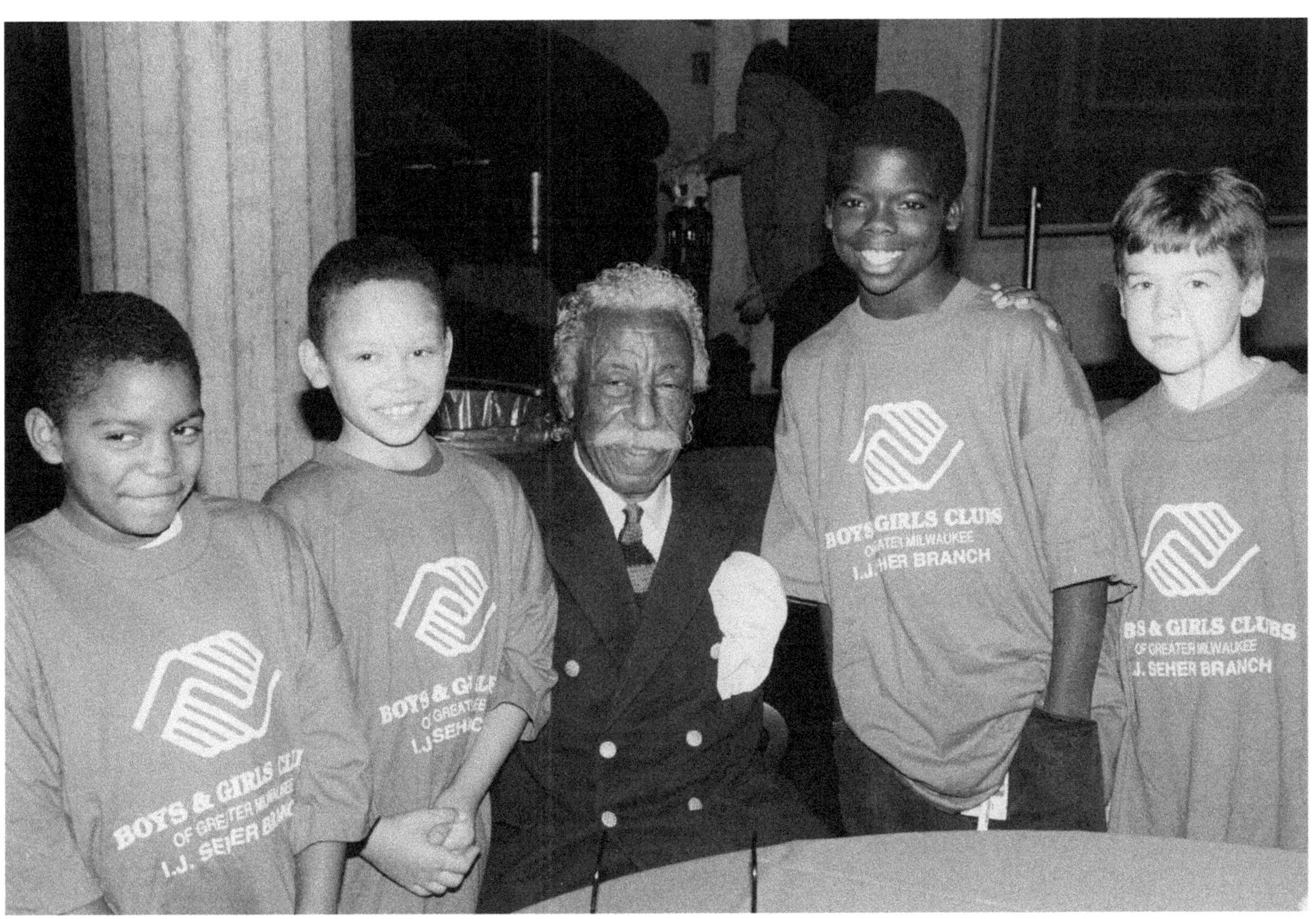
BOYS & GIRLS CLUBS
OF GREATER MILWAUKEE
I.J. SEHER BRANCH

Boys & Girls Clubs of Greater Milwaukee Members Jumping Rope, 1999

A group of Boys & Girls Clubs members jump Double Dutch at a club gymnasium.

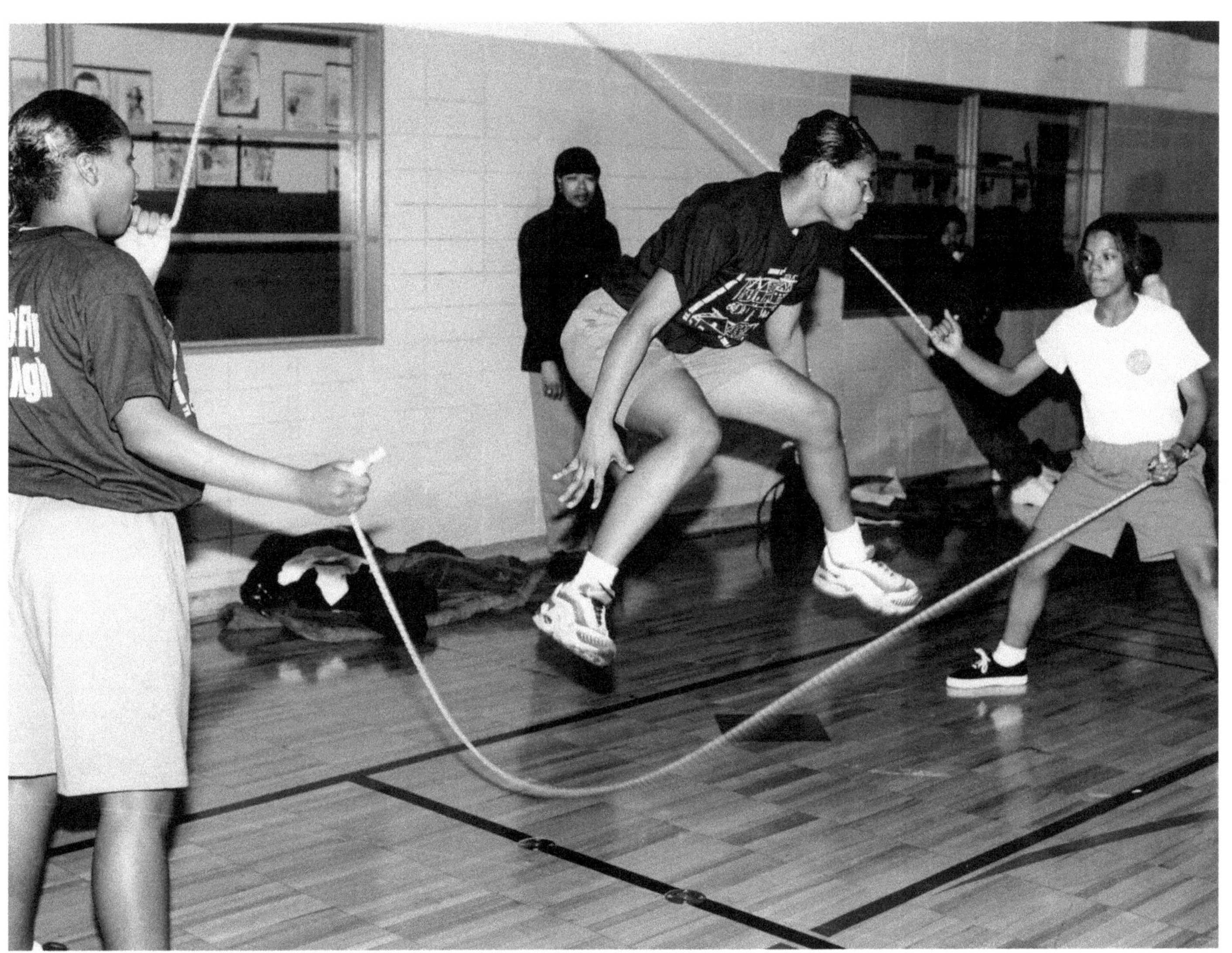

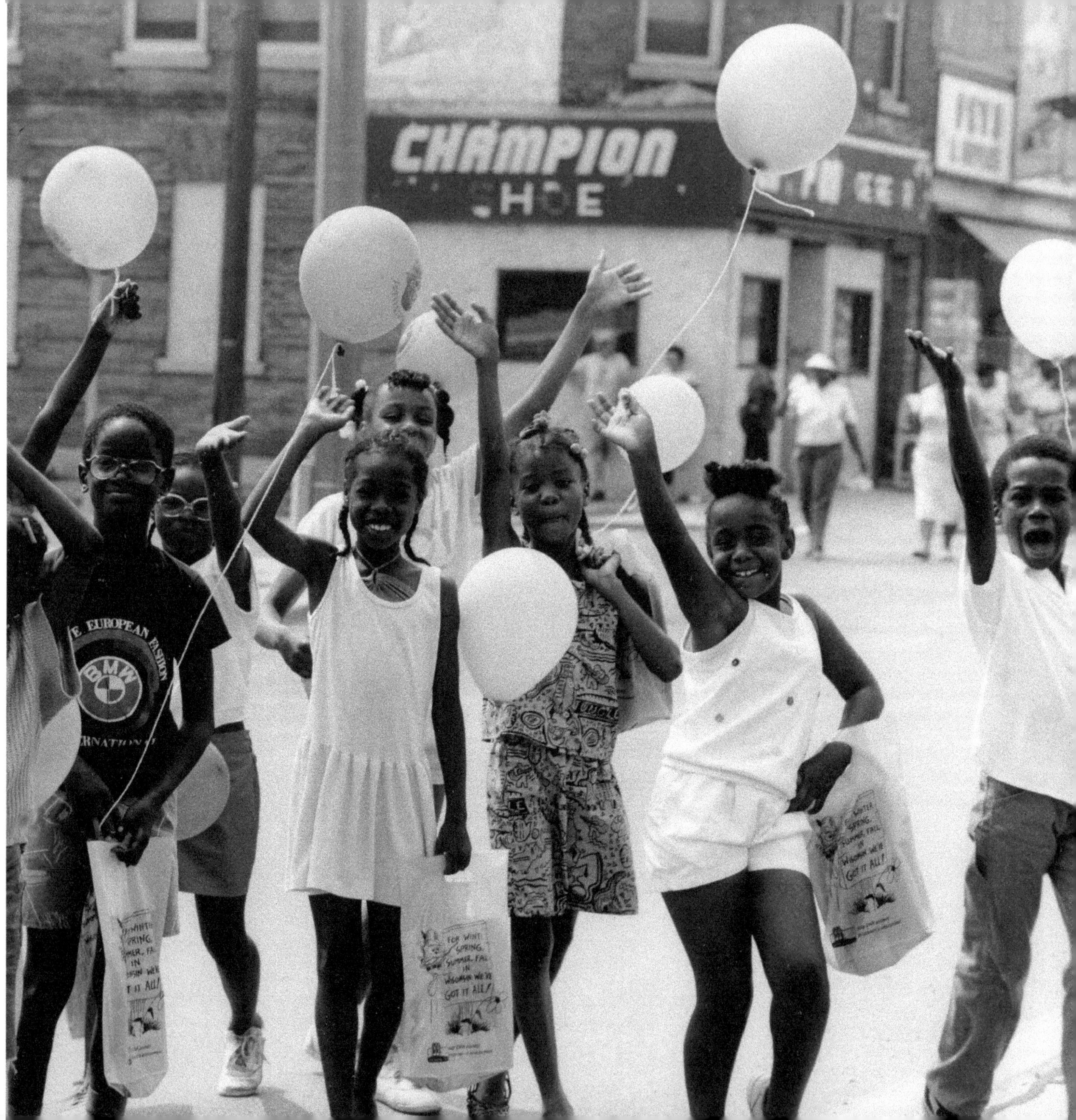

CHAMPION
SHOE
E EUROPEAN FASHION
BMW
INTERNATIONAL
FOR WINTER, SPRING, SUMMER, FALL IN WISCONSIN WE'VE GOT IT ALL!

Community

Milwaukee's Black population grew significantly in the decades immediately following World War II, during a period referred to by historians as the Great Migration. The population ballooned from 21,772 in 1950, to 62,458 in 1960, and then to 105,088 in 1970. These numbers highlight the continued movement of Black southerners to Milwaukee, due largely to the industrial employment opportunities still available in the "Machine Shop of the World." As an urban and industrial destination, Milwaukee and its neighborhoods were transformed by the influx of African Americans from the South, many of whom found stable economic opportunities. However, even as some Black people benefitted from labor opportunities in the Cream City, others faced economic challenges as the city began its steep industrial decline (beginning in 1970). Nonetheless, as Milwaukee's Black population increased and African Americans redefined the city's geopolitical and economic landscapes, local businesses, schools, and neighborhoods were forever changed.

Milwaukee Firefighter Ed Boatman, 1988

Milwaukee firefighter Ed Boatman cools off using a fire hose on the night of August 18, 1988, when three explosions and a five-alarm fire went off at the Felix Bandos Waste Material Company warehouse (1132 S. Barclay St.). More than 100 firefighters came to the scene. Five were injured due to the presence of unreported chemicals in the warehouse. One month prior to the fire, federal regulations were put in place requiring businesses to report hazardous substances to the Fire Department. Compliance with the regulations could have prevented injuries and lessened the intensity of the fire.

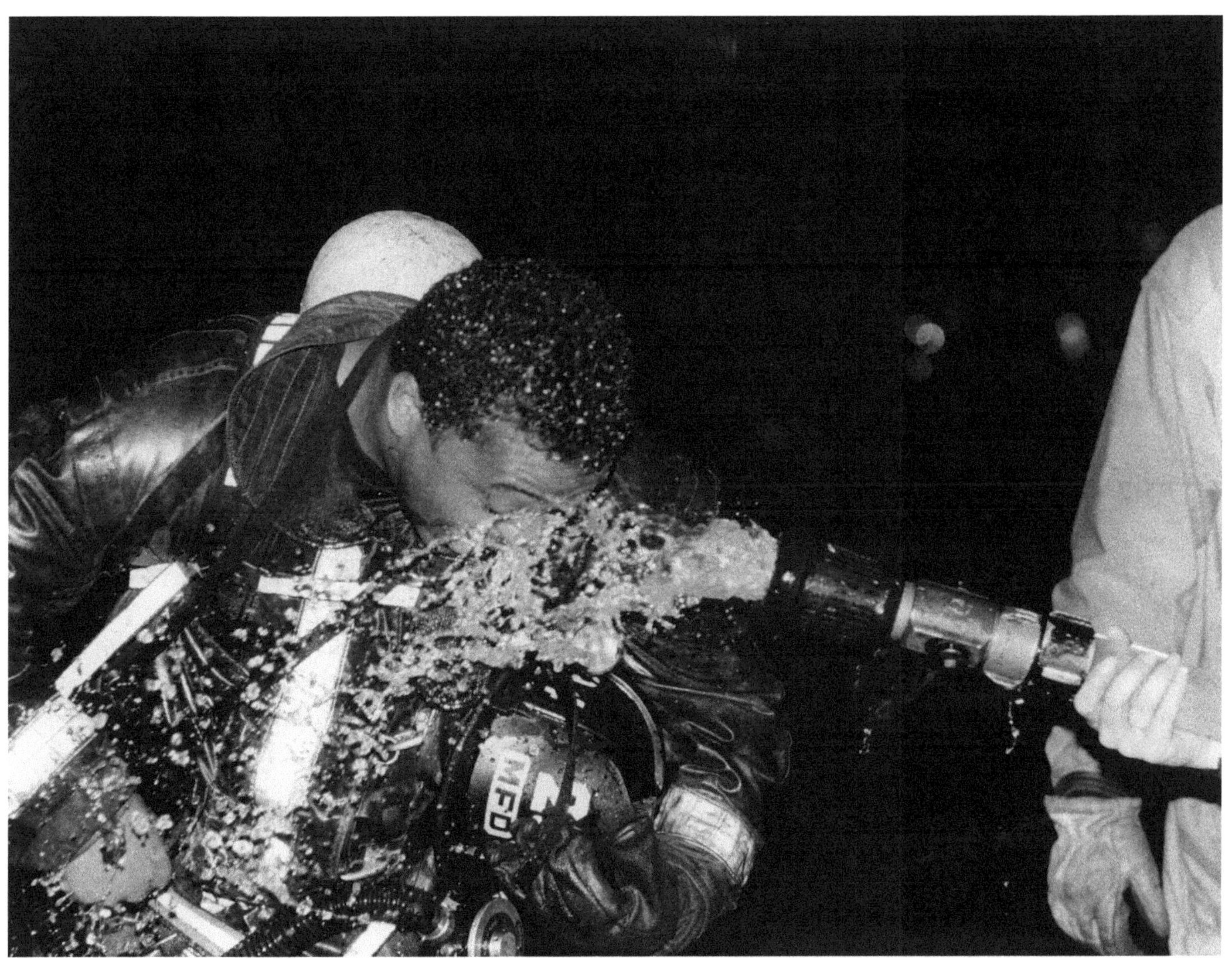

Children with Balloons, 1987

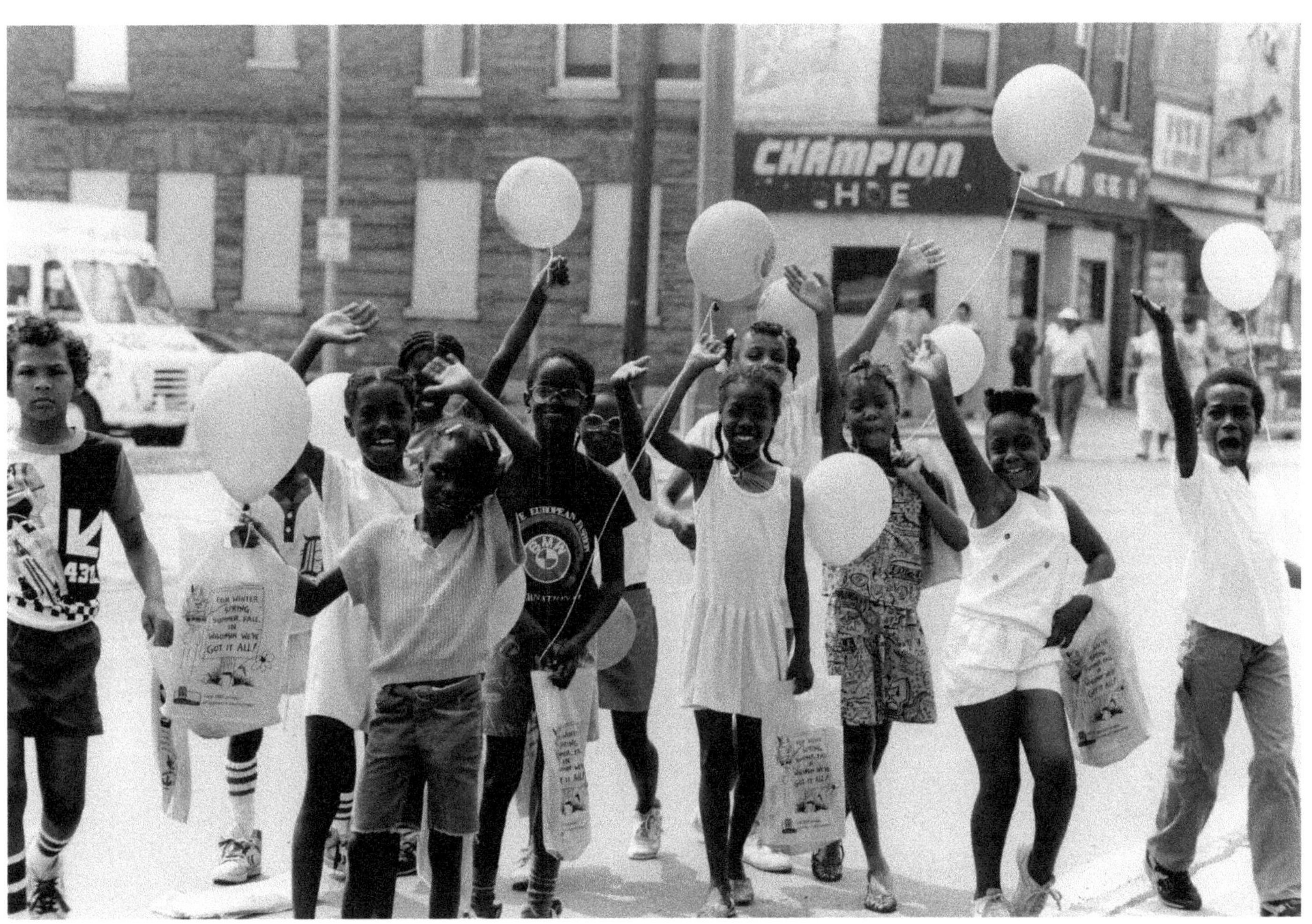

CHAMPION
SHOE

***Milwaukee Storyteller, Folklorist, and Historian Tejumola Ologboni
on African World Festival Float, 1988***

African World Festival was an annual celebration of African and African American culture held at Henry Maier Festival Park on Milwaukee's lakefront from 1983 until 2013. The festival was revived in 2018 with the establishment of Black Arts Fest MKE.

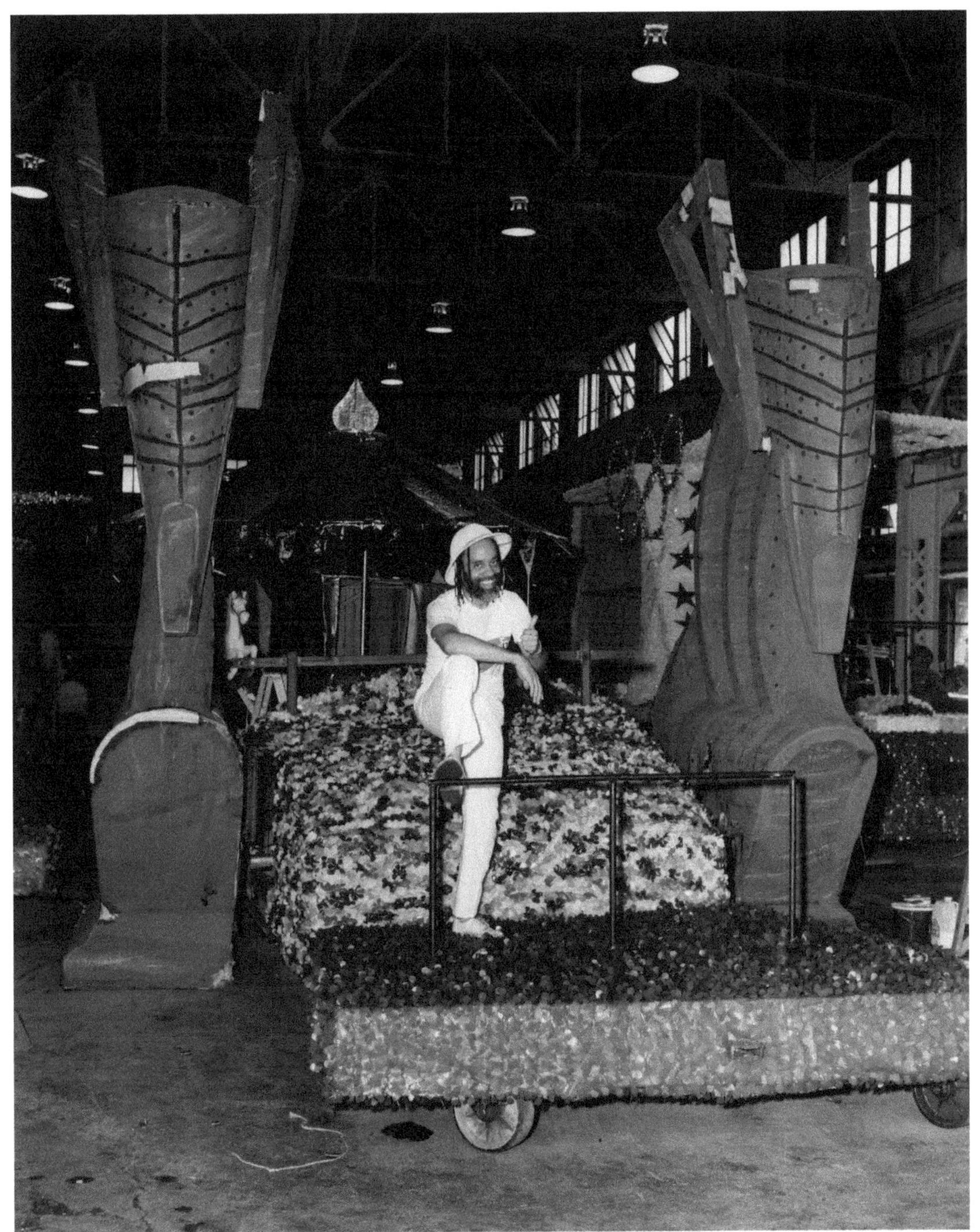

Women and Children, 1989

Women and children smile for the camera during a Milwaukee street festival.

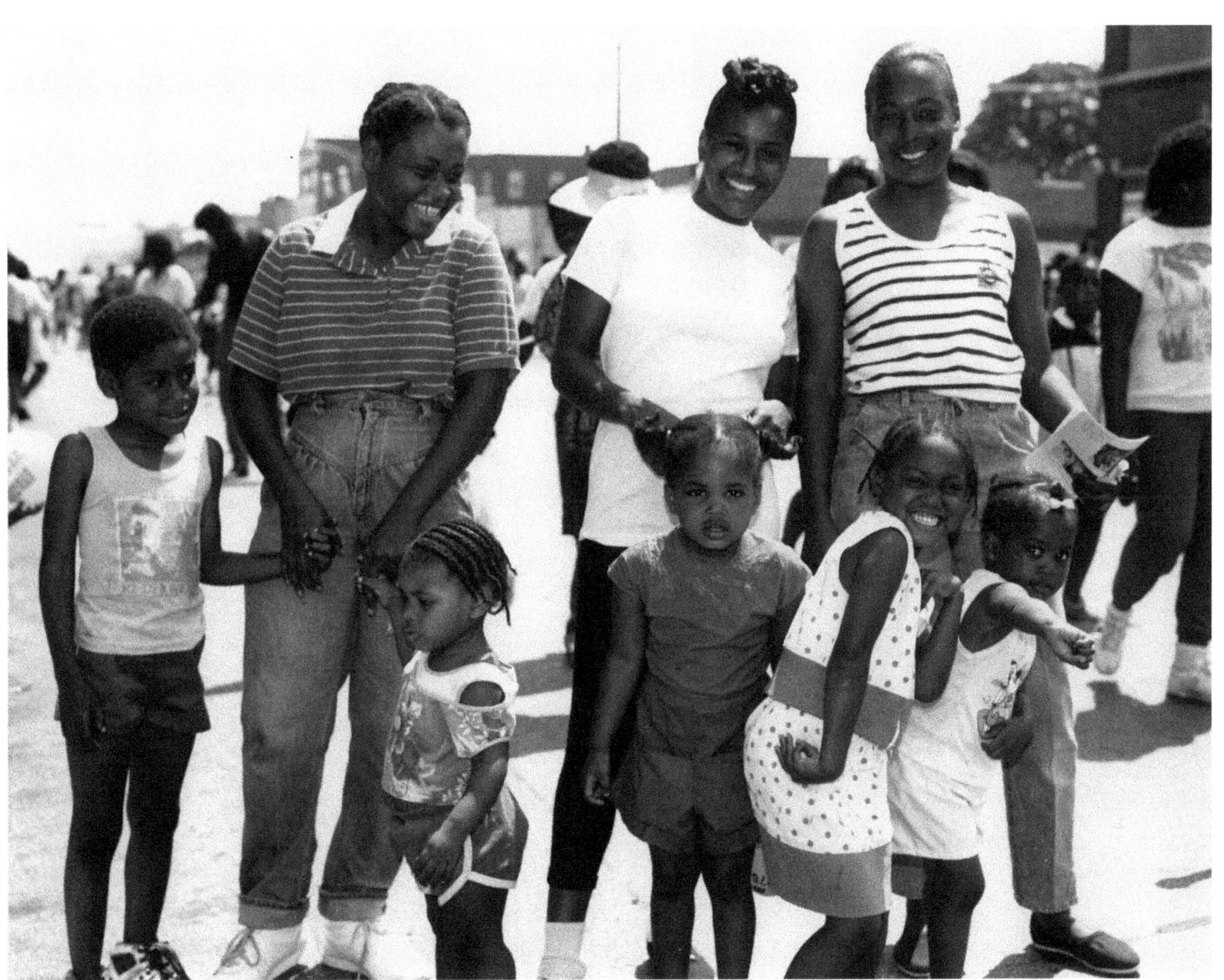

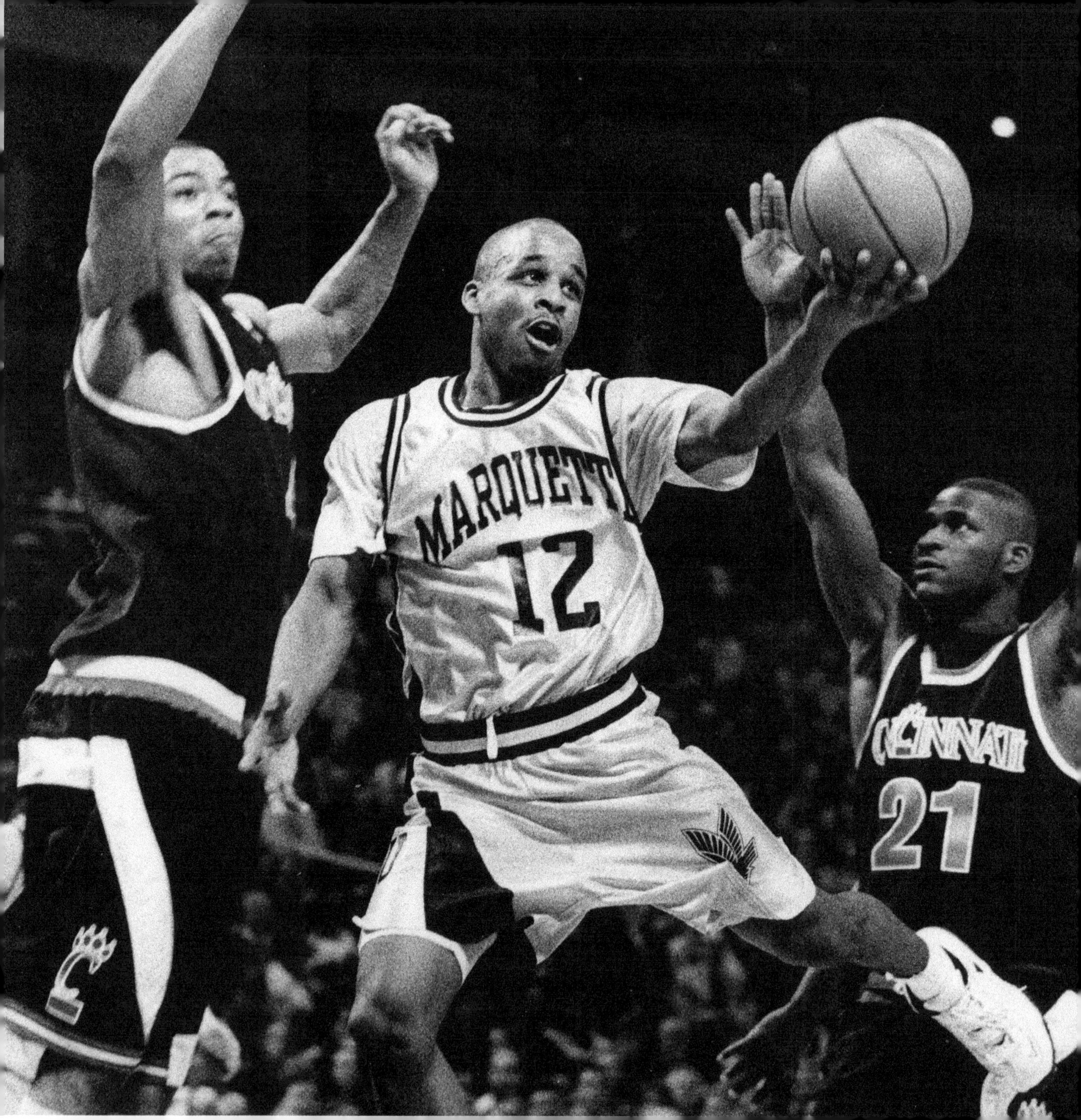
MARQUETTE
12
CINNATI
21

Sports

Milwaukee and Wisconsin have a rich professional and collegiate sports history that includes the presence of remarkable African American athletes and personalities. Their impact on and off the field and court highlights the role sports and sports figures play in ongoing debates about racial equality, racial identity, and other social and political issues. Some outstanding Milwaukee athletes that represent this history of social activism include Hank Aaron, Kareem Abdul-Jabbar, Bob Lanier, Glenn Robinson, Dwyane Wade, Giannis Antetokounmpo, and George Hill.

Black Milwaukee is also associated with a number of lesser-known individuals who have used sports to support local communities—youth and children's groups in particular. Milwaukee is home to former Negro League players who founded and coached Beckum-Stapleton Little League, the longest-running Black Little League Baseball organization outside of the South. Jimmy Banks, a former soccer star and coach of the Milwaukee School of Engineering soccer team, brought the sport to hundreds of Milwaukee youth. He received the posthumous honor of Custer Stadium being renamed Jimmy Banks Memorial Stadium.

Kareem Abdul-Jabbar, 1988

During a pregame ceremony in 1988 in Milwaukee, the Bucks presented Kareem Abdul-Jabbar with a Harley Davidson motorcycle to honor his retirement from basketball. Abdul-Jabbar set various records for the Milwaukee Bucks during the 1970s and received many prestigious personal awards. His achievements while playing for the Bucks include three MVP awards, an NBA Finals MVP award, five All-NBA selections, and the scoring champion of 1971 and 1972. Equally important is Abdul-Jabbar's commitment to activism and racial justice work off the court. Born Ferdinand Lewis Alcindor, Abdul-Jabbar changed his name while in Milwaukee to reflect his conversion to Islam and to shed a name that was connected to the legacy of slavery. Today he is known not only as an NBA champion, but also as a lifelong champion of racial and social justice.

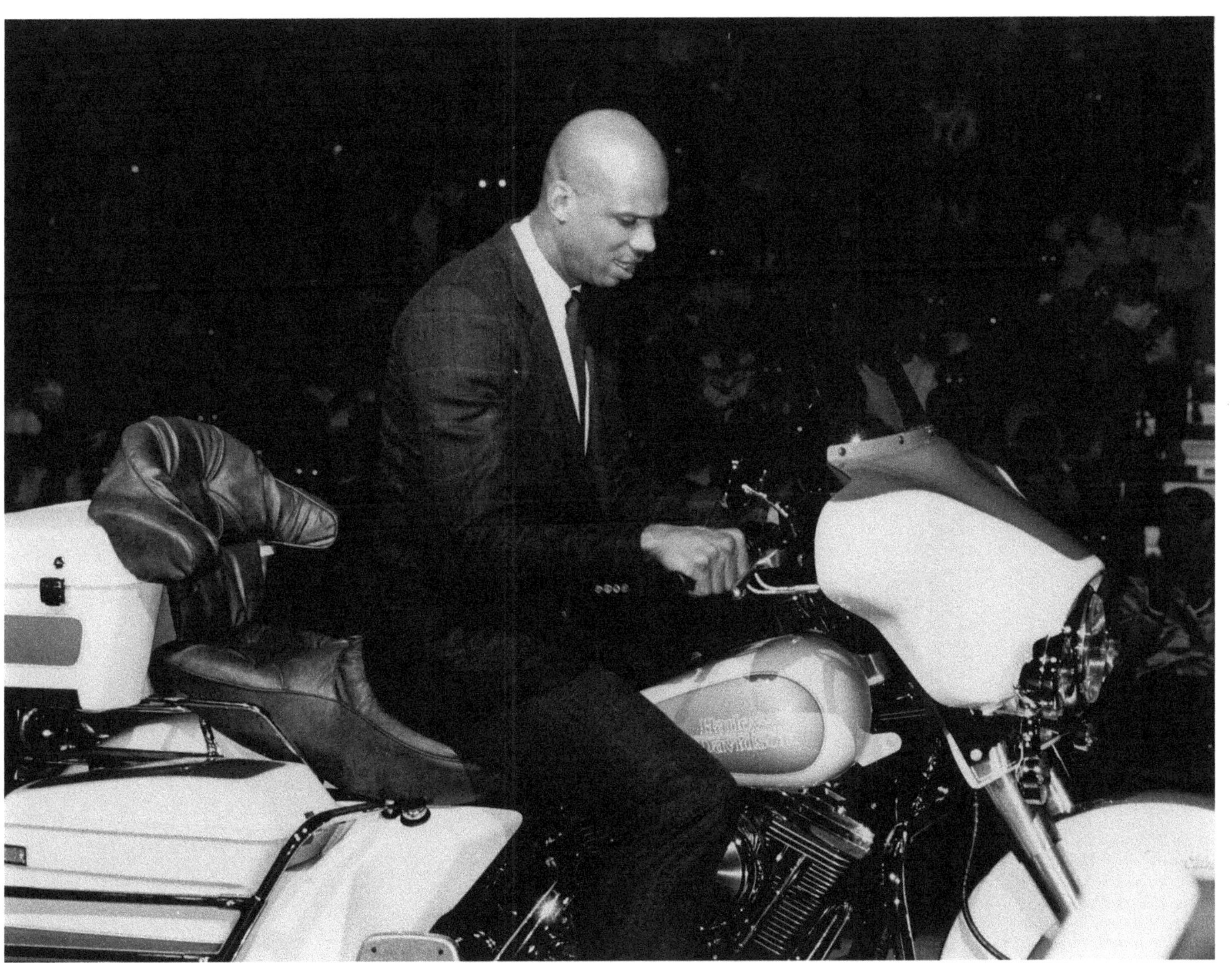

Vin Baker and Glenn Robinson, 1995

Vin Baker (left) and Glenn Robinson (right) were two of the most versatile players on the Milwaukee Bucks for a number of years. Baker, who played with the Bucks from 1993 to 1997, played for other teams before returning to Milwaukee in 2018 as an assistant coach for the Bucks. He is also an outspoken advocate for addressing the harms of addiction, having personally dealt with alcoholism. Robinson, who played with the Bucks from 1994 to 2002, had numerous career highs before retiring in 2005 due to injuries.

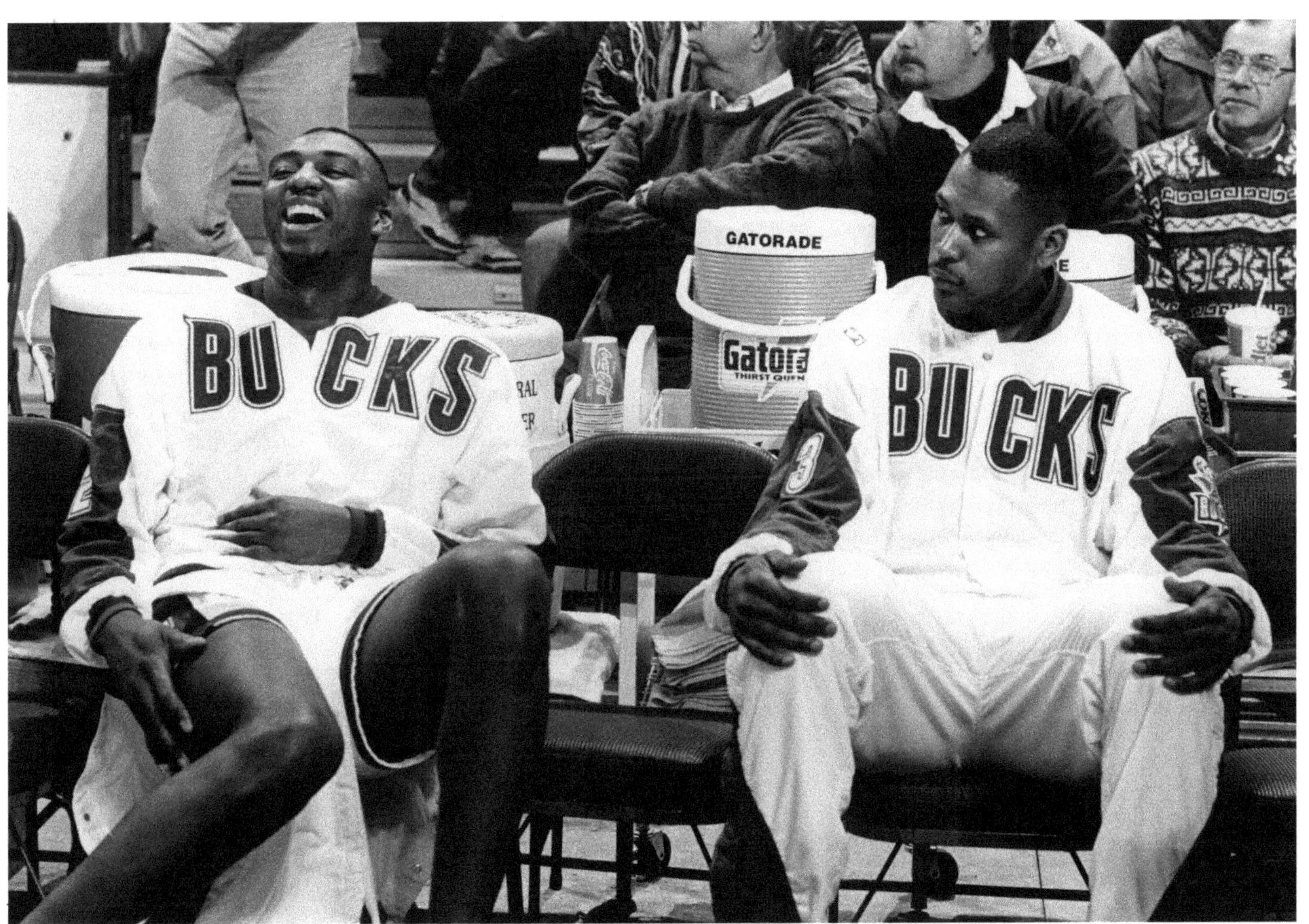

BUCKS
BUCKS
GATORADE
Gatorade
THIRST QUEN

Tiger Woods's First Pro Swing, 1996

Only 20 years old and still in his undergraduate studies at Stanford University, Eldrick "Tiger" Woods was not yet at professional golfer status when he accepted a sponsor's exemption to play in the 1996 PGA Tour's Greater Milwaukee Open at Brown Deer Park Golf Course. He had already won three U.S. Amateur Championships prior to this tournament, which began in late August that year. Here Tennessen captures Woods's professional debut, where he finished in a tie for 60th place.

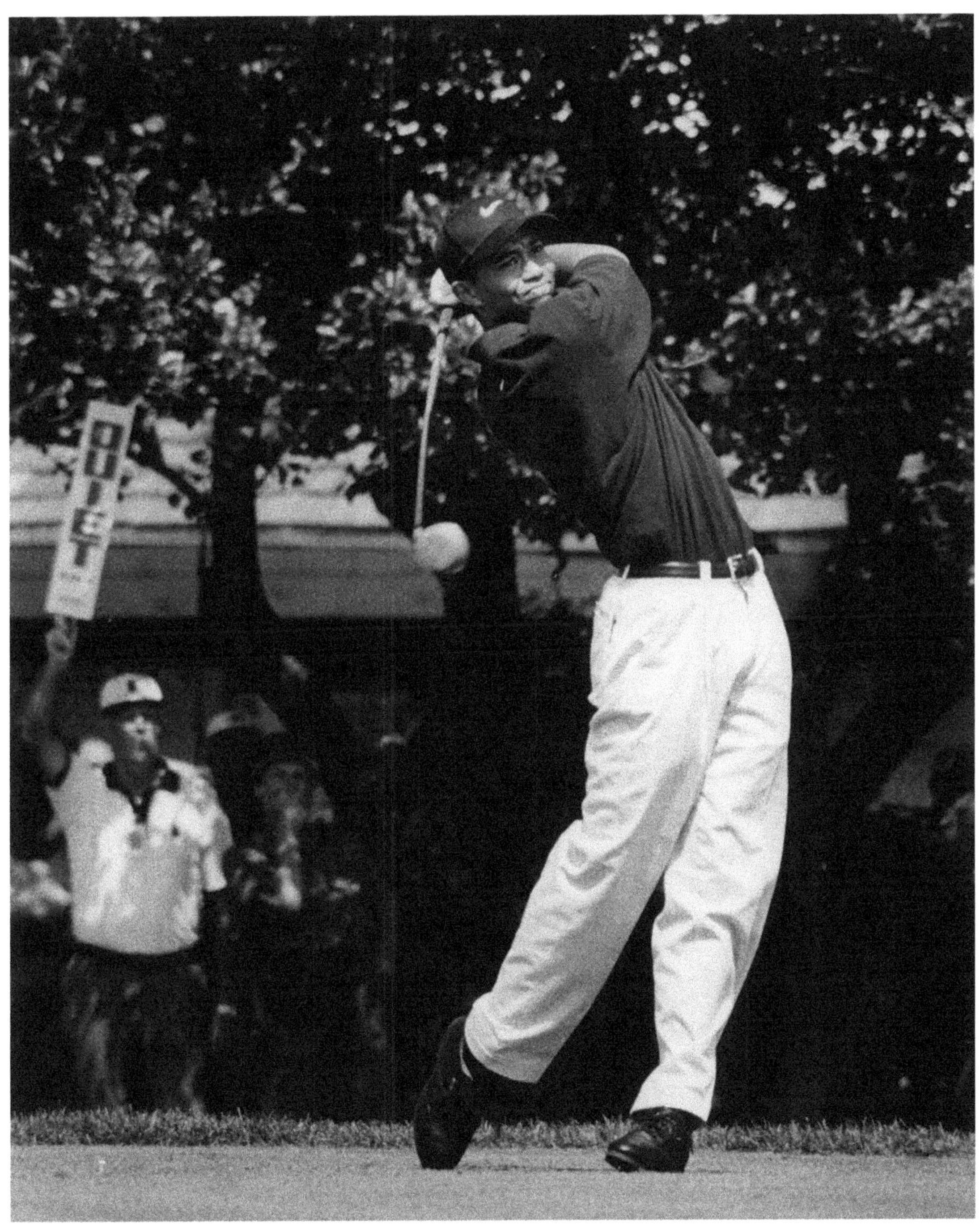
QUIET

Aaron Hutchins (Marquette University, #12) Against
Melvin Levett (University of Cincinnati, #21), 1997

Aaron Hutchins played for Marquette from 1994 through 1998. He endured a number of hardships after leaving Marquette but continued to pursue a college diploma. He received a degree in Communication from Marquette in 2019, 20 years after first departing the University. Levett played for University of Cincinnati from 1995 through 1999. He set the school's record for three-point field goals in a single game (10) against Eastern Kentucky.

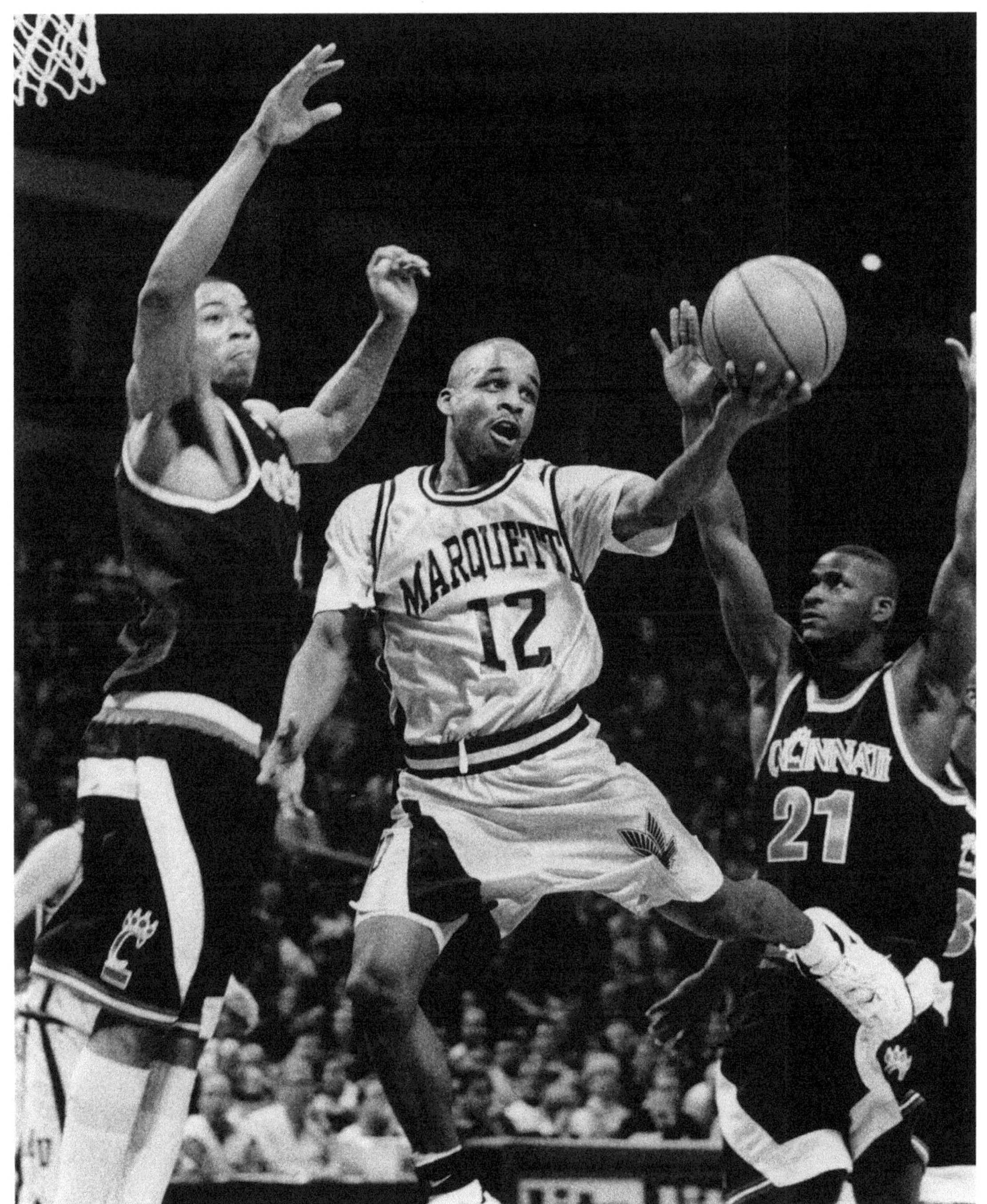

Black Baseball in Milwaukee–National Negro League Players, 1998

In 1998, an event was held in partnership with the Milwaukee Public Museum to honor Black baseball in Milwaukee's past. Dennis Biddle (center of the image closest to the sign) is a former Negro League player and currently runs the Yesterday's Negro League Players Foundation. He also was a coach in the Beckum-Stapleton Little League (one of the oldest African American run Little League organizations in the country), which was founded by James Beckum, another former Negro League player.

The Milwaukee Bears were Milwaukee's only Negro League Baseball team. The team folded after one partial season in 1923, due to financial constraints. Biddle, the Milwaukee Brewers, and local historians have worked hard to keep the memory and contributions of the Bears alive.

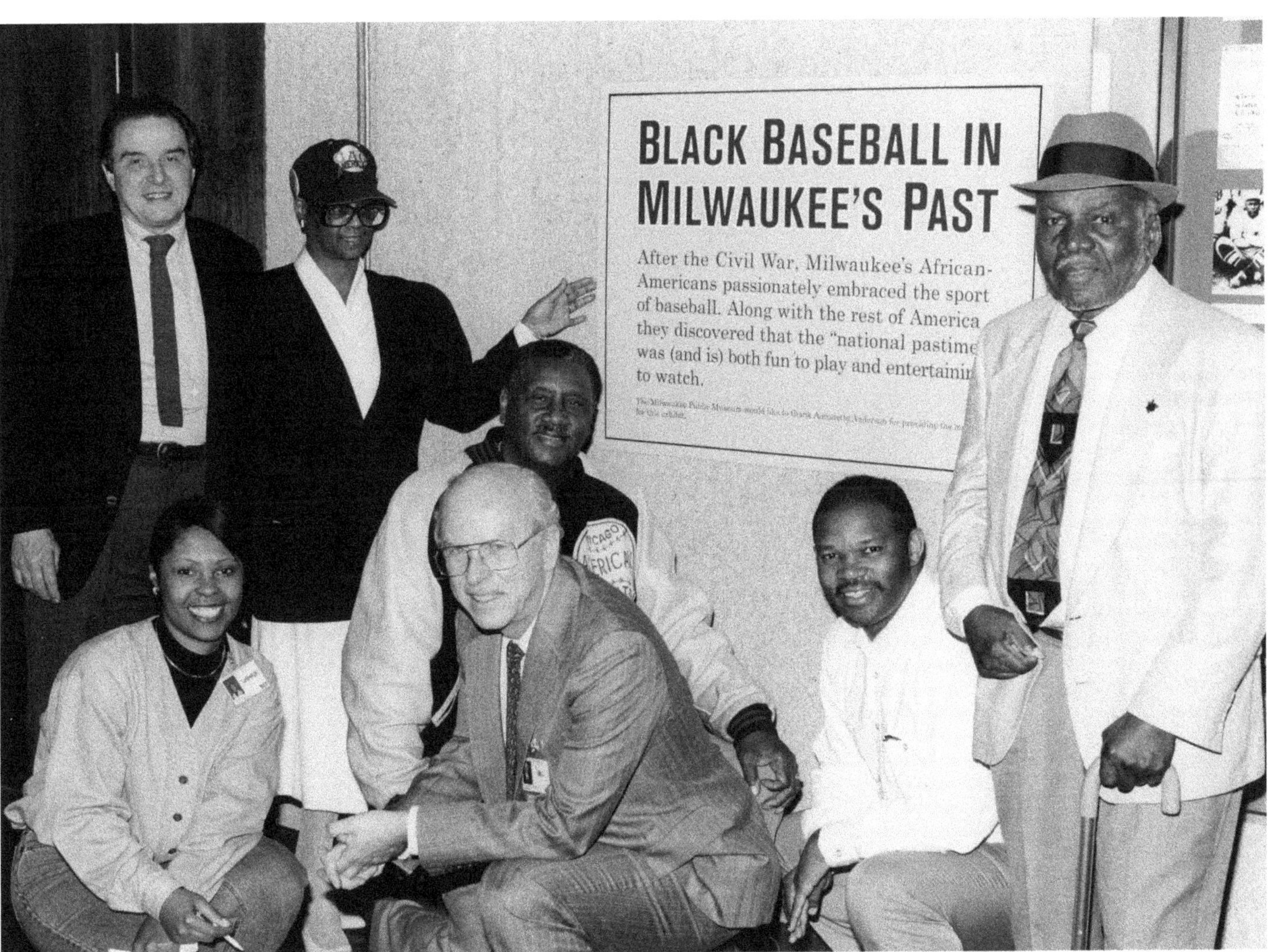
BLACK BASEBALL IN MILWAUKEE'S PAST
After the Civil War, Milwaukee's African-Americans passionately embraced the sport of baseball. Along with the rest of America they discovered that the "national pastime" was (and is) both fun to play and entertaining to watch.

Ray Allen (left) and Allen Iverson (right), 2001

Ray Allen of the Milwaukee Bucks against Allen Iverson of the Philadelphia 76ers in Game 6 of the 2001 NBA playoffs. The Bucks won the game to tie the series 3 to 3. Philadelphia went on to win the series 4 games to 3.

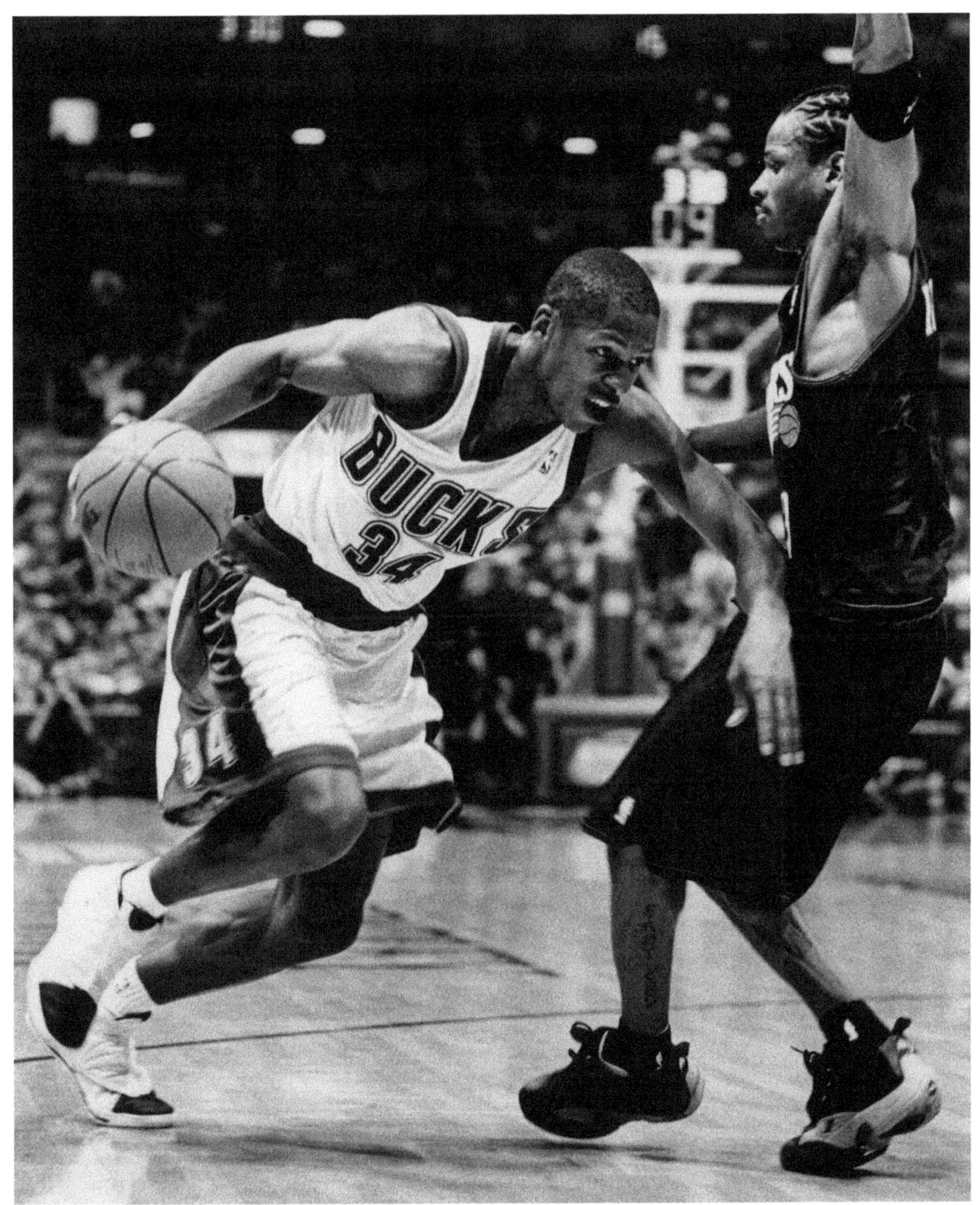

Dwyane Wade, 2003

Even though Dwyane Wade only played for Marquette University for three years (2000–2003), he has cemented a legacy as one of the most decorated Marquette Men's Basketball players in the university's history. After leaving Marquette, Wade went on to be drafted fifth overall in the NBA, was inducted into the Naismith Basketball Hall of Fame, and has pursued numerous philanthropic causes within Milwaukee and beyond.

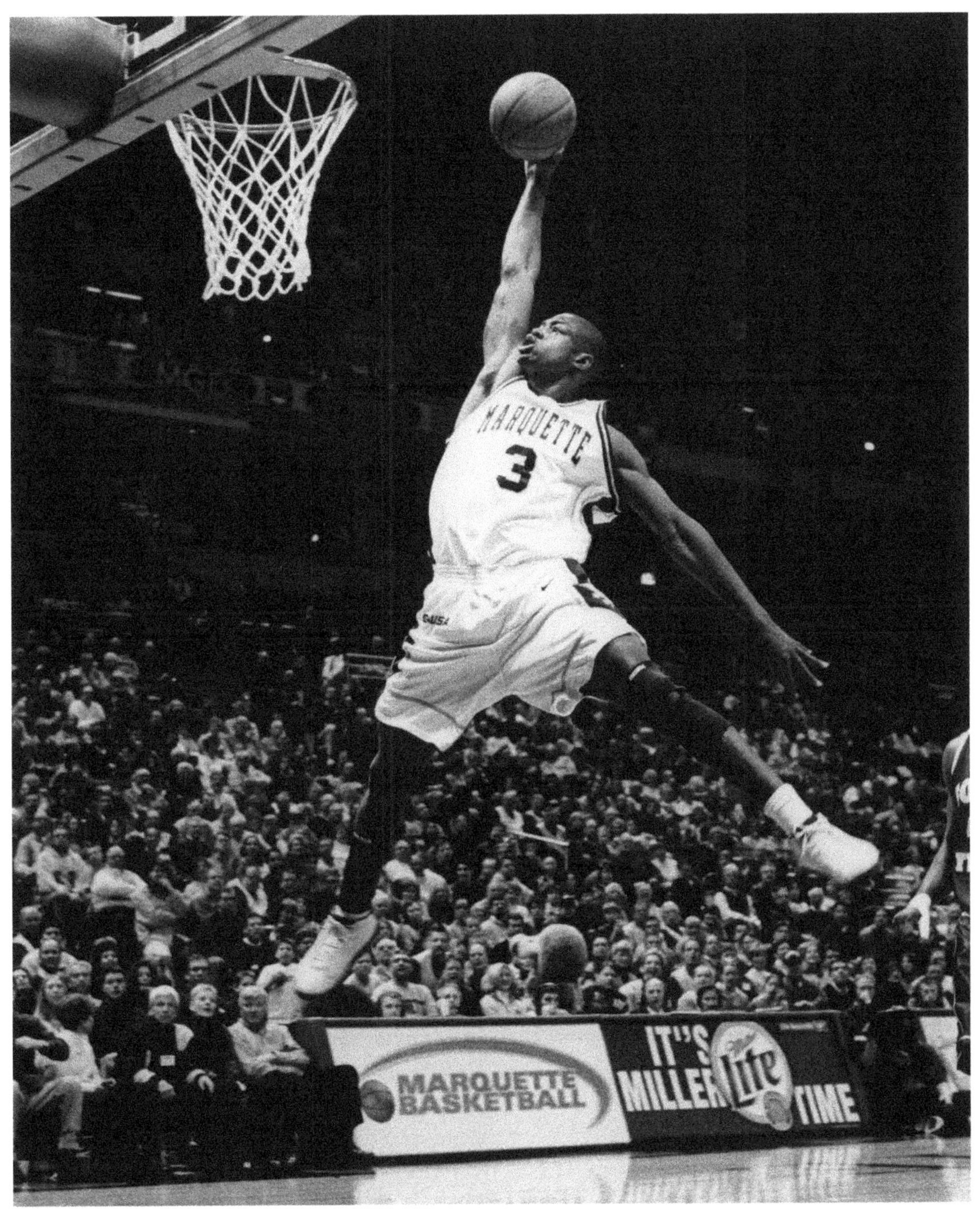

MARQUETTE
3
MARQUETTE BASKETBALL
IT"S MILLER Lite TIME

Mo Williams (Milwaukee Bucks) and Dwyane Wade (Miami Heat), 2004

Mo Williams of the Milwaukee Bucks goes up against former Marquette University star
Dwyane Wade (playing for the Miami Heat). Williams played for the Bucks from 2004 to 2008.
Wade played for the Heat from 2003 to 2016.

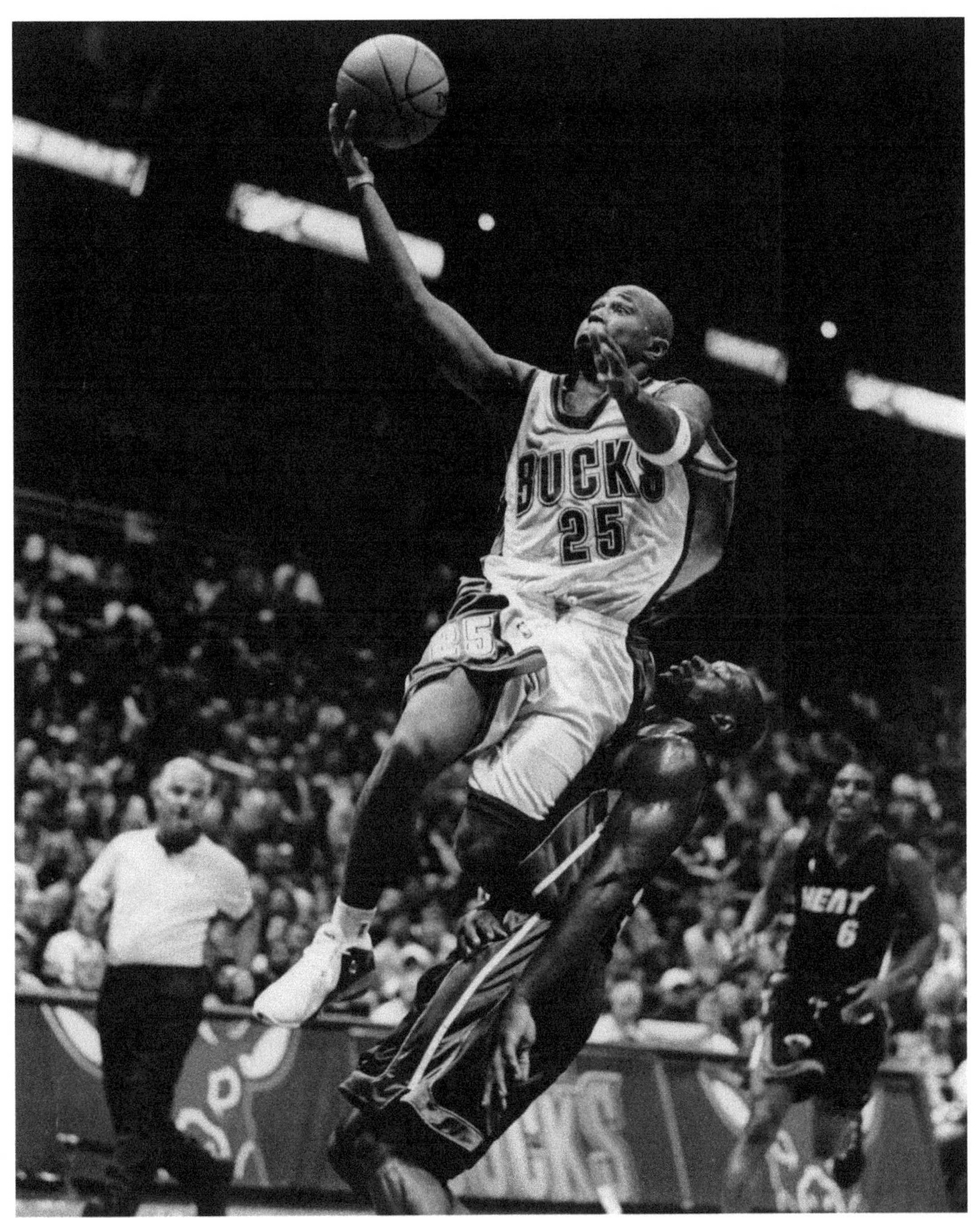

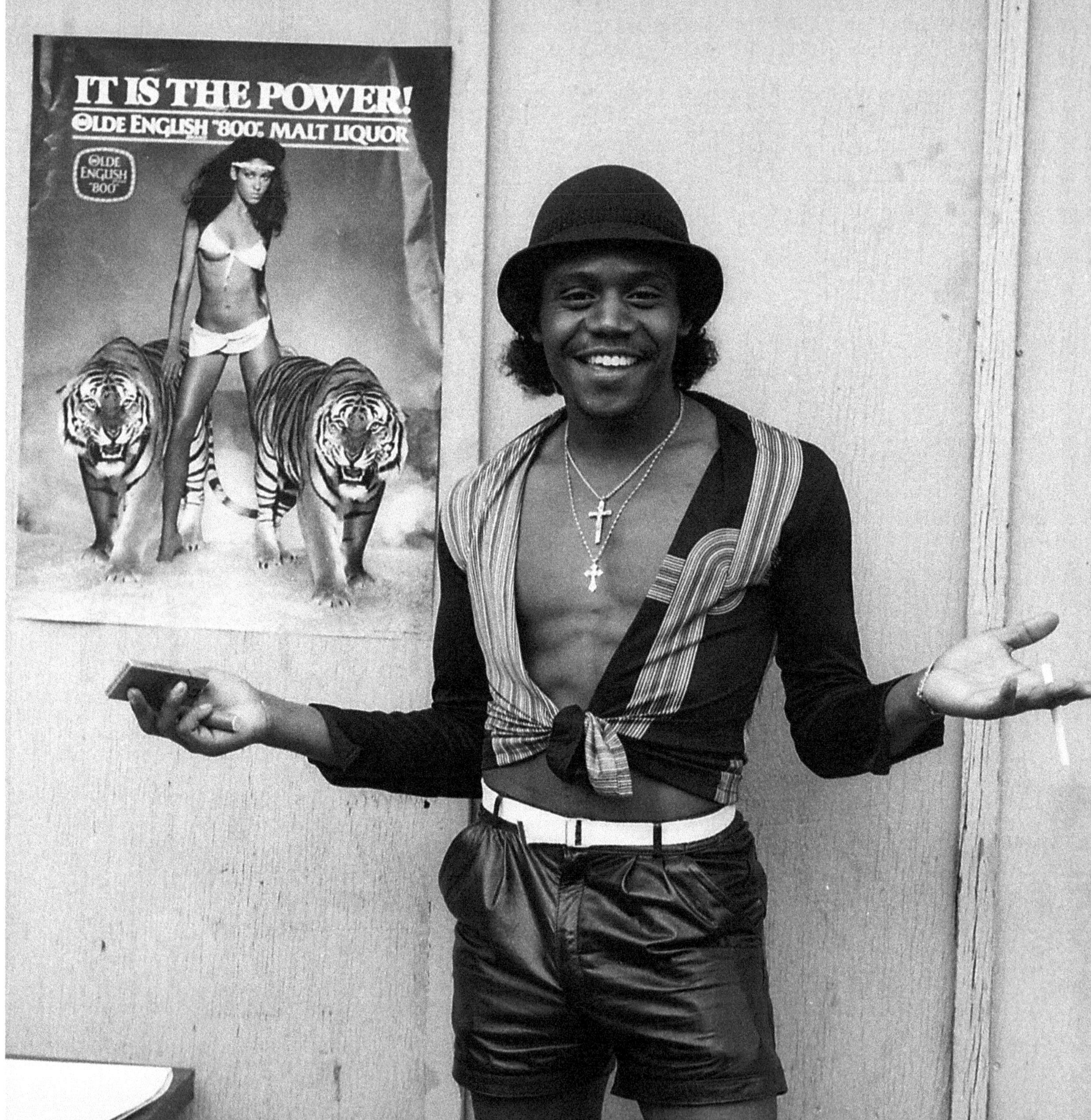

IT IS THE POWER!
OLDE ENGLISH "800" MALT LIQUOR
OLDE ENGLISH "800"

Appendix: Street Photography 101

In preparing for the Haggerty show, I surveyed Dad's personal collection of black and white negatives. I estimated that he photographed and developed at least 275,000 35mm negatives, plus several thousand additional medium format and large format negatives.

It's difficult to appreciate today how much work is involved in developing this much film, and then printing any meaningful fraction of it. At best, it takes around 45 minutes of work to develop a single roll of 24 or 36 exposures. Lab work needs to be meticulous and all variables accounted for. Chemicals are brought up to the right temperature, the negatives are bathed for a set amount of time, and agitation needs to be regular and repeatable. As chemicals are used up, they are discarded, or in Dad's case, the use was noted so that the development time could be compensated for the next time that chemical batch was used.

Looking over so many of these old photos and negatives, I was amazed to see how many photos were never printed. That's not necessarily a bad thing. The first lesson I ever learned from Dad in the darkroom was the importance of the wastebasket. Use it early and often, and only show your best work.

Nevertheless, I think it's really interesting to look over the following roll of film. The remaining pages are direct scans of a single roll of film from Dad's collection. Most of the photos are from the June 19, 1985 celebration of Juneteenth Day. This event takes place on Martin Luther King Jr Drive, in the area of Wright Street and close to the Northcott Neighborhood house, the event's sponsor.

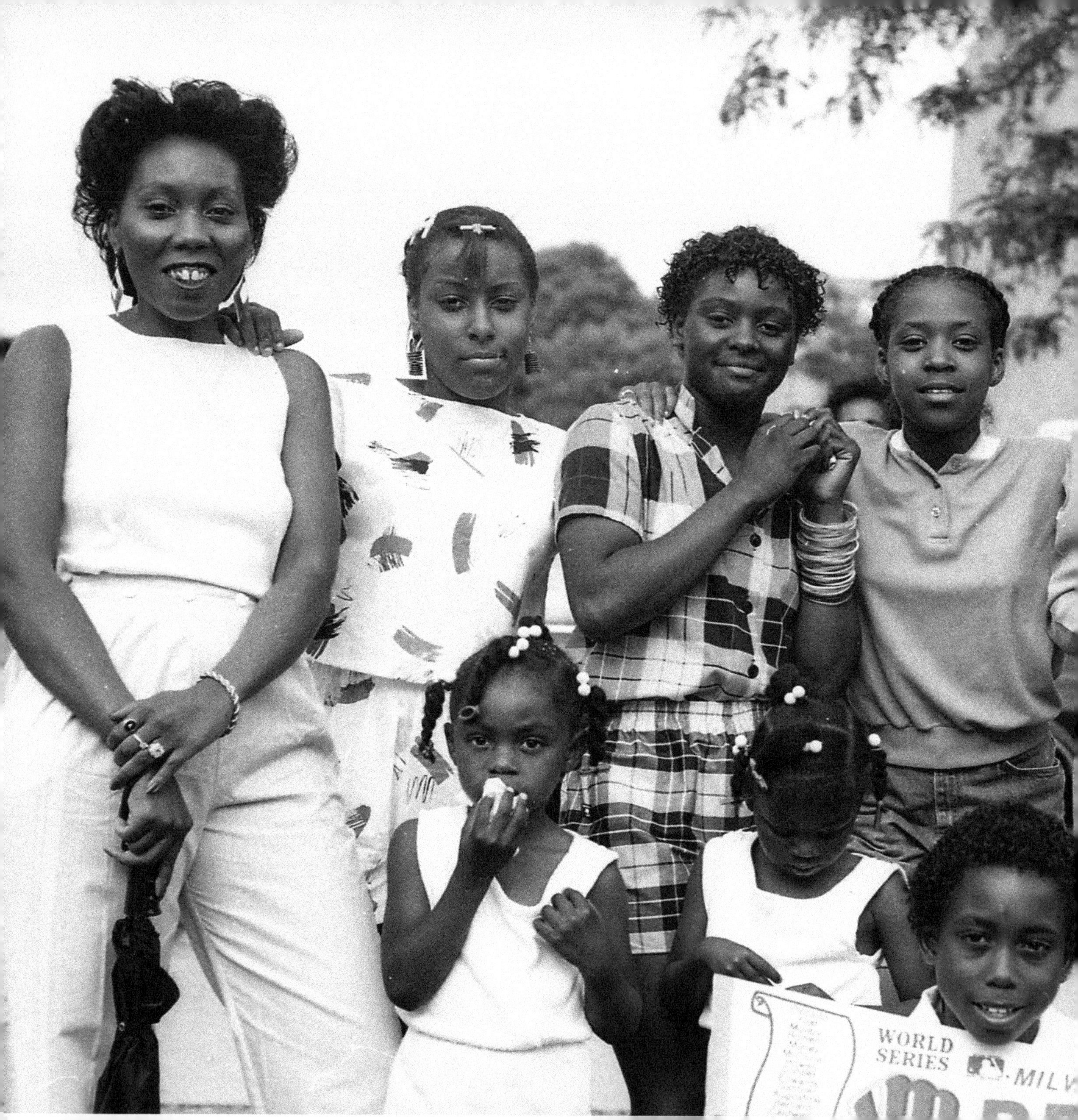

WORLD
SERIES
MILV

While most photographers would be happy to have one decent photo per roll, or even less, there were three photos selected from this single roll of film for the Haggerty show. There are at least three more photos that could have been, if Dad had even bothered to print them. For me, this roll represents a really, really good day of street photography. It feels like everyone is willing to stop and smile for Dad's camera, which was most likely a Leica M with a 50mm Summicron lens. The film was Kodak Panatomic X, a slow but extremely fine-grained film. You can see different versions of the same photo as subjects gather and willingly give the gift of their visible images. Any photographer would be grateful to have a roll filled with this many intriguing and beautiful images.

Did Dad rush home to the darkroom after one of his greatest days as a photographer, impatient to see his photos? No. The 36-exposure roll of film was not finished, and no thrifty photographer would ever waste those remaining images. He waited for something else to photograph, in this case, a weekend fire drill for the Fox Point Fire Department, where Dad was a volunteer firefighter for almost 40 years. Once the last little bit of film was exposed, then it was ready for the darkroom.

—Editor

5060
KODAK SAFETY FILM 5060
KODAK SA

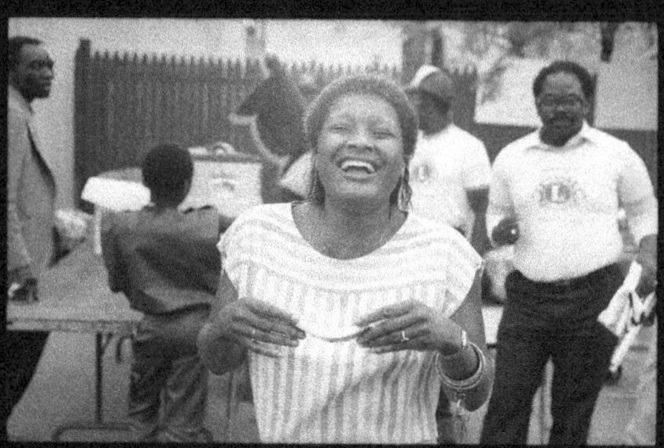
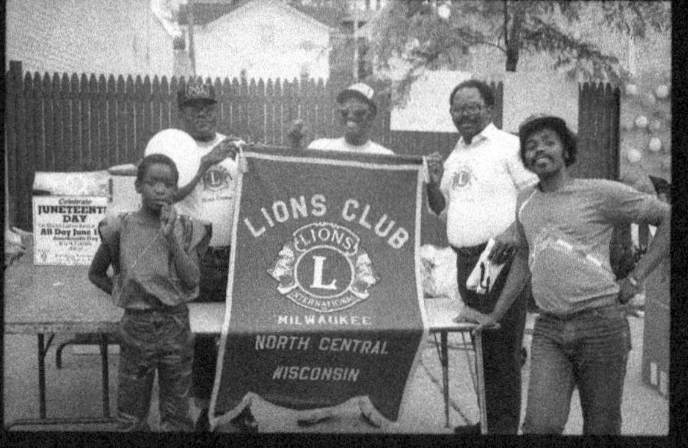
Celebrate
JUNETEENTH
DAY
All Day June 1
LIONS CLUB
LIONS
L
INTERNATIONAL
MILWAUKEE
NORTH CENTRAL
WISCONSIN
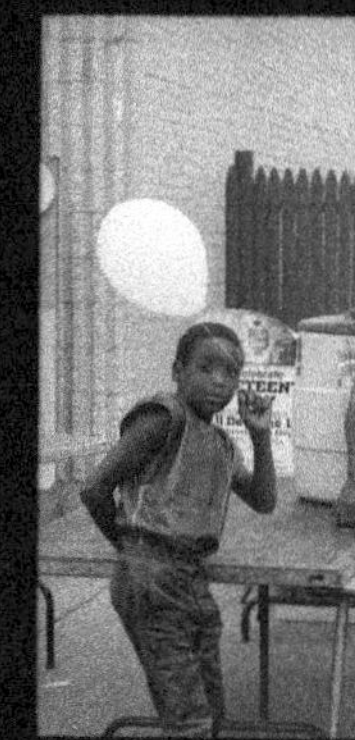

→ 2   → 2A   → 3   → 3A

KODAK SAFETY FILM 5060   KODAK SAFETY FILM 5060

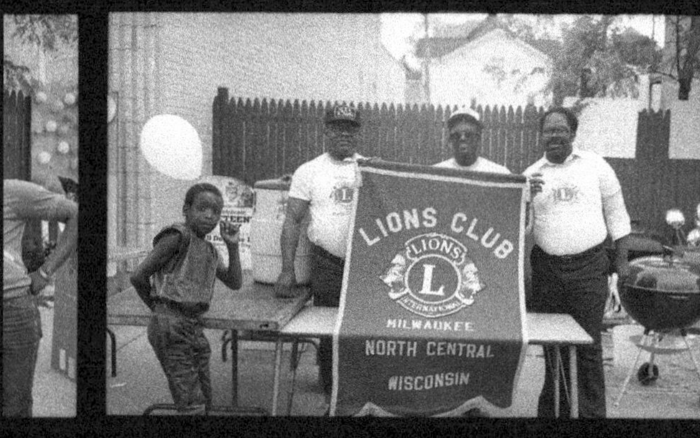
LIONS CLUB
LIONS
L
INTERNATIONAL
MILWAUKEE
NORTH CENTRAL
WISCONSIN
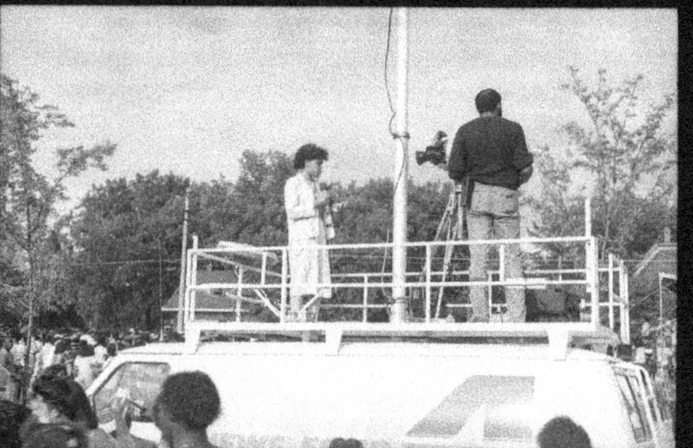
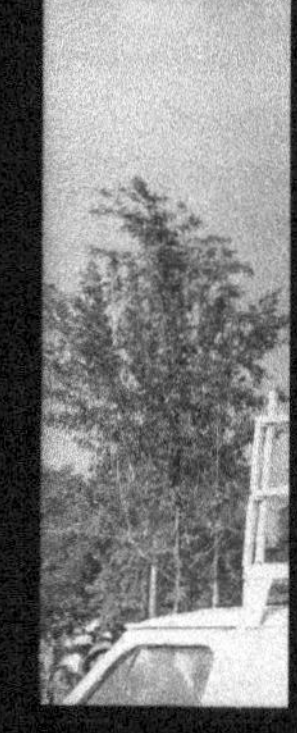

→ 3A   → 4   → 4A   → 5   → 5A

TY FILM 5060   KODAK SAFETY FILM 5060

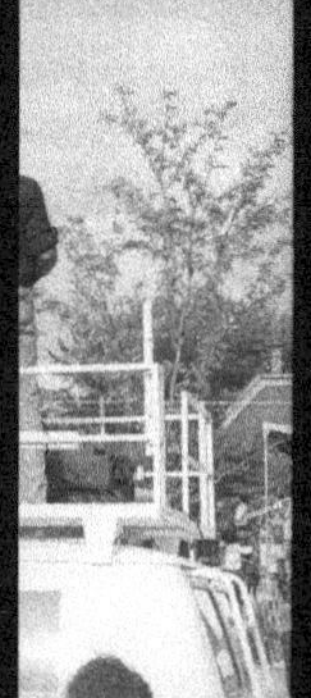
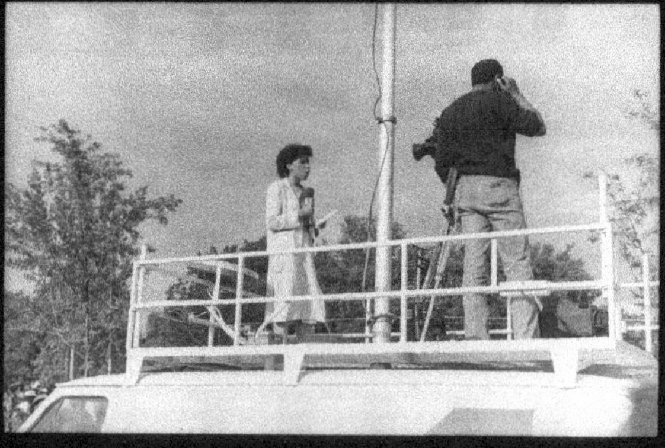
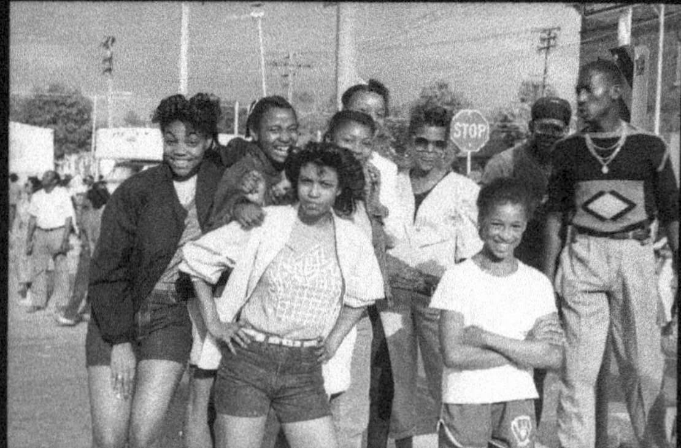
STOP

→ 5A   → 6   → 6A   → 7   → 7A

KODAK SAFETY FILM 5060

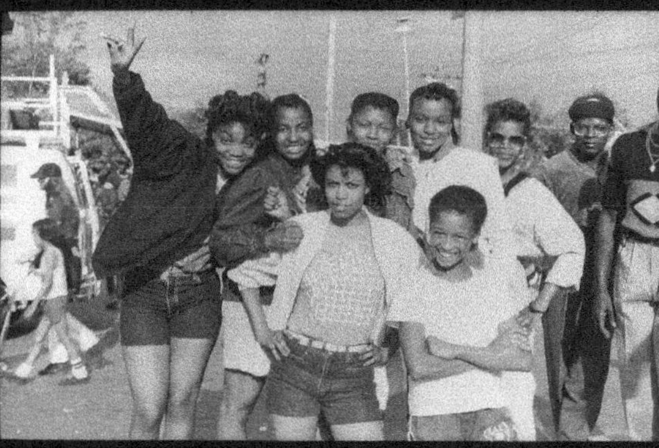 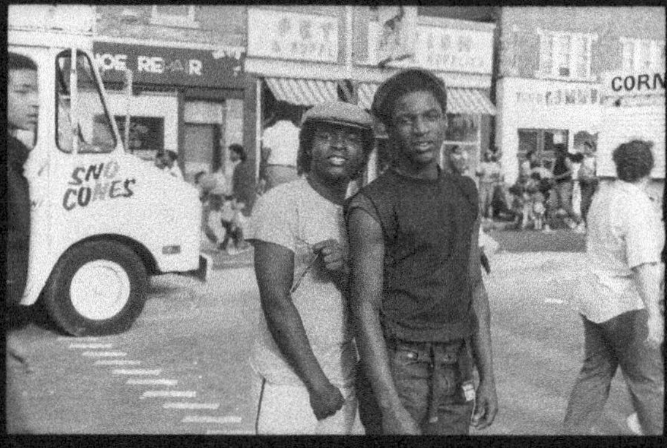 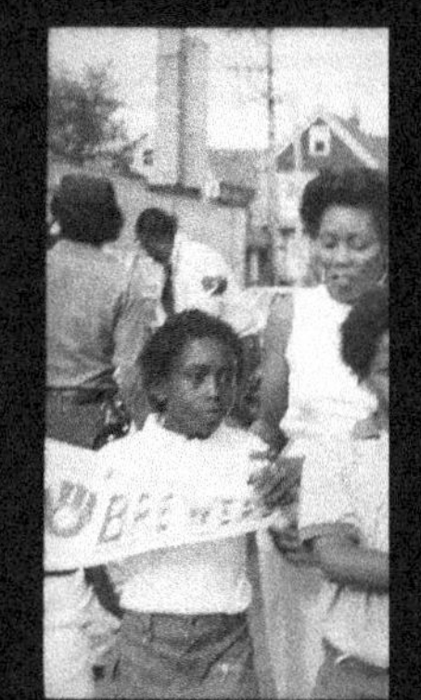

→ 8   → 8A   → 9   → 9A   →

FILM 5060   KODAK SAFETY FILM 5060   KODAK

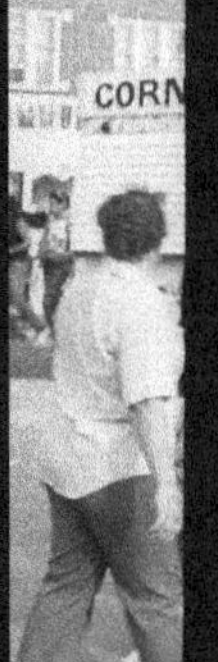 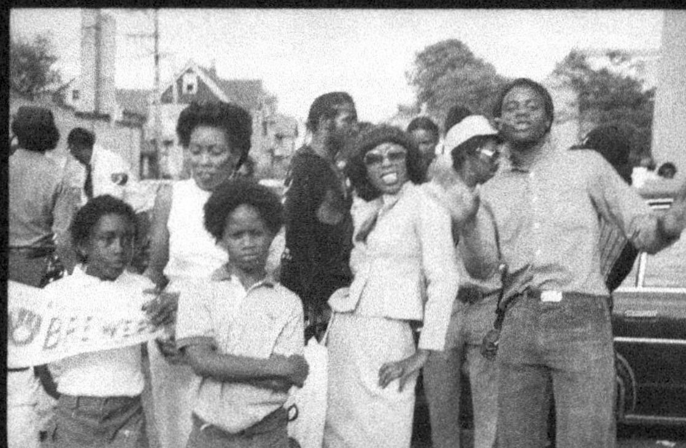 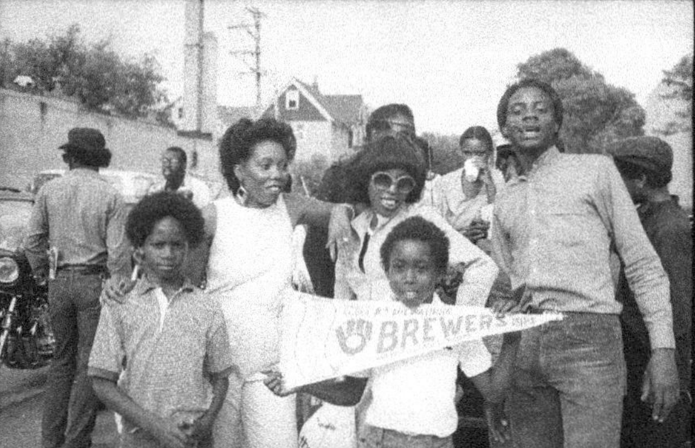 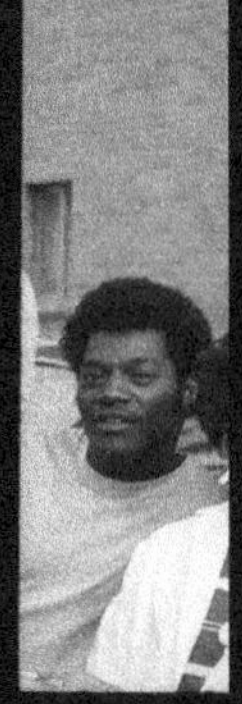

→ 9A   → 10   → 10A   → 11   → 11A

KODAK SAFETY FILM 5060   KODAK SAFETY FILM

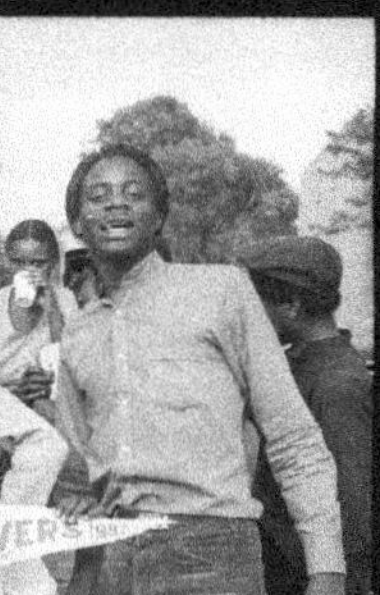 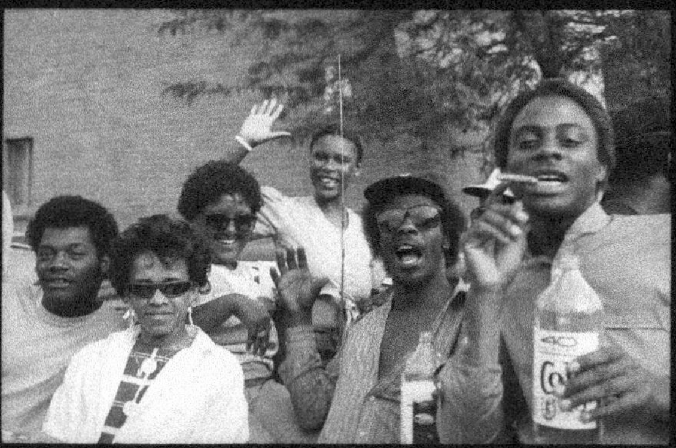 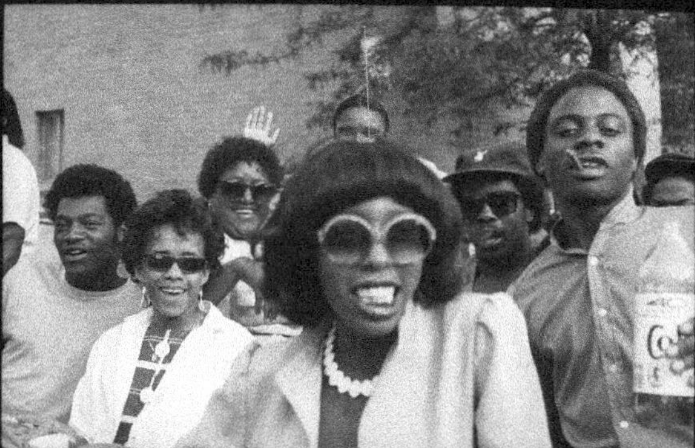

→ 11A   → 12   → 12A   → 13   → 13A

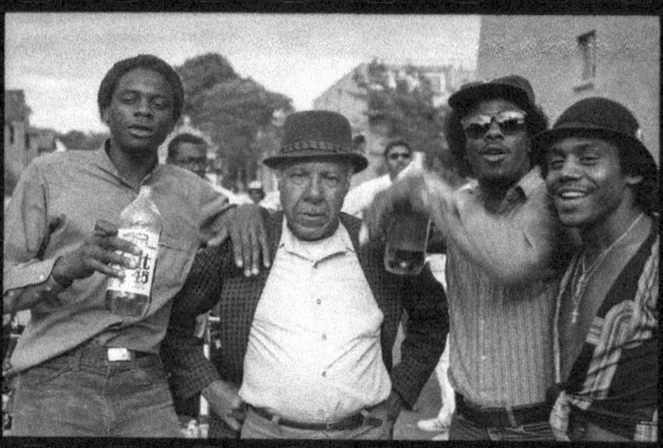
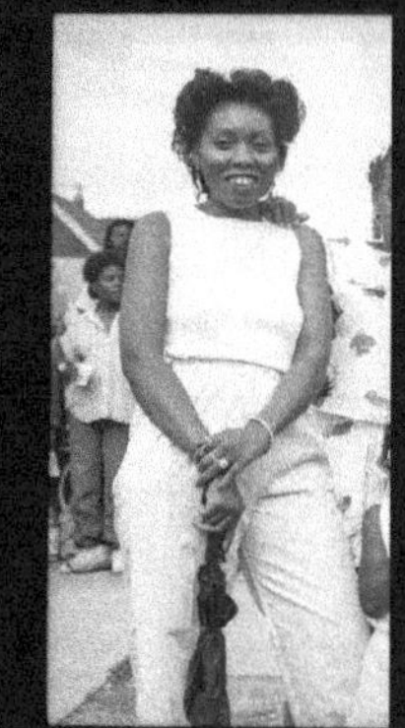

→14   →14A   →15   →15A   →
KODAK SAFETY FILM 5060   KODAK SAFETY FILM 5060

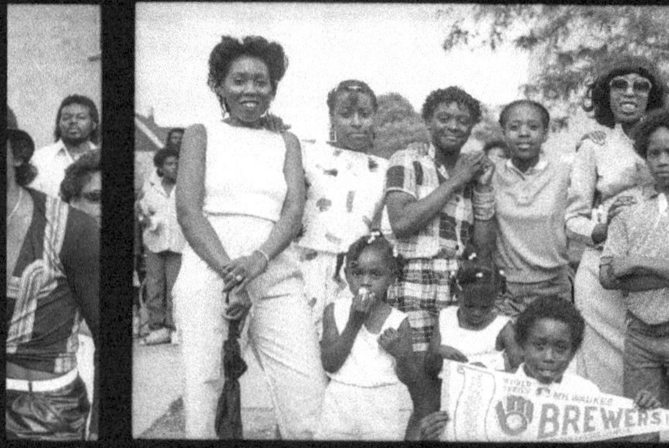
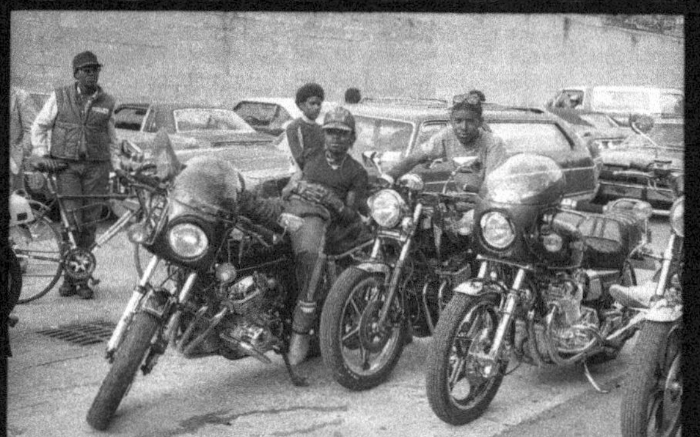
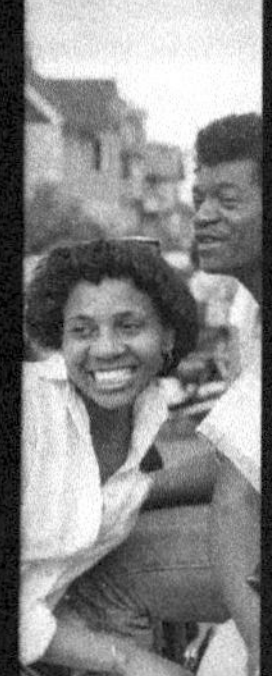

5A   →16   →16A   →17   →17A
TY FILM 5060   KODAK SAFETY FILM 5060   K

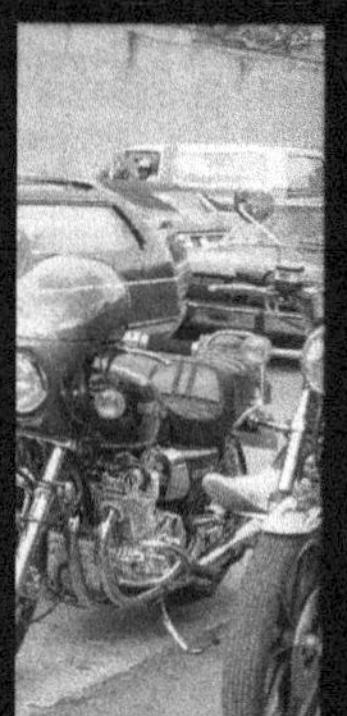
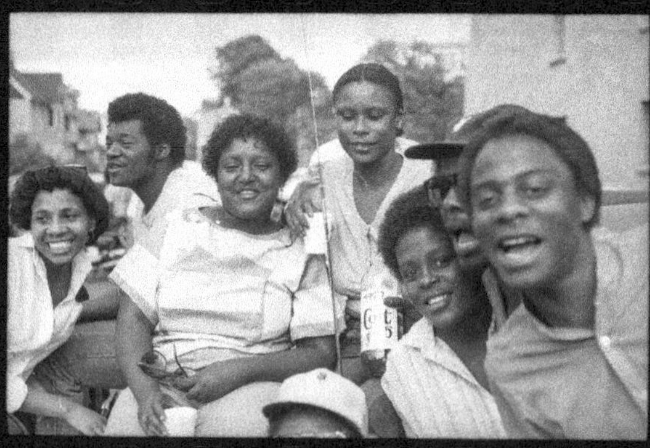
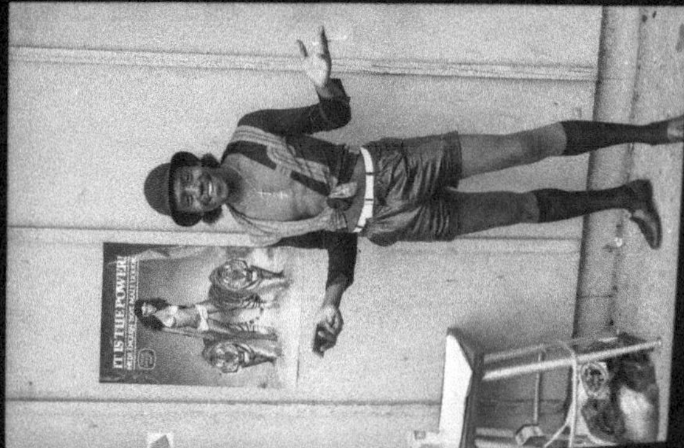

→17A   →18   →18A   →19   →19A

ODAK SAFETY FILM 506C
KODAK SAFETY FILM 5060

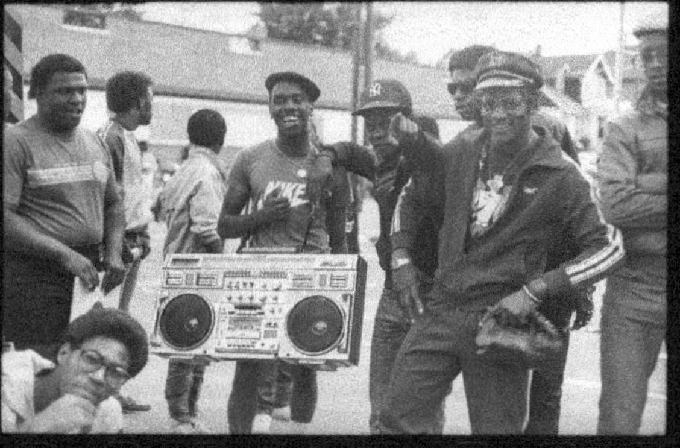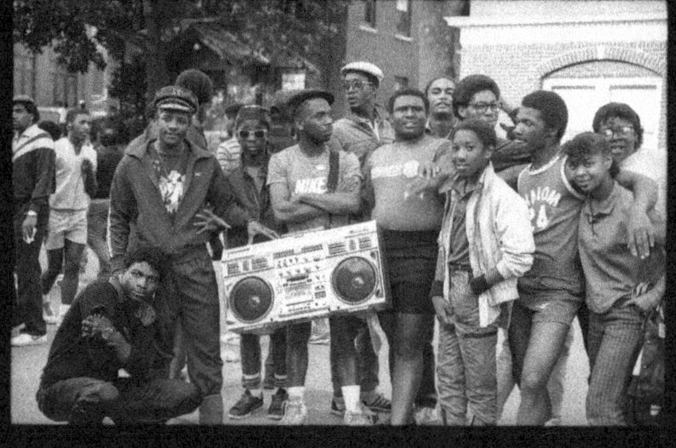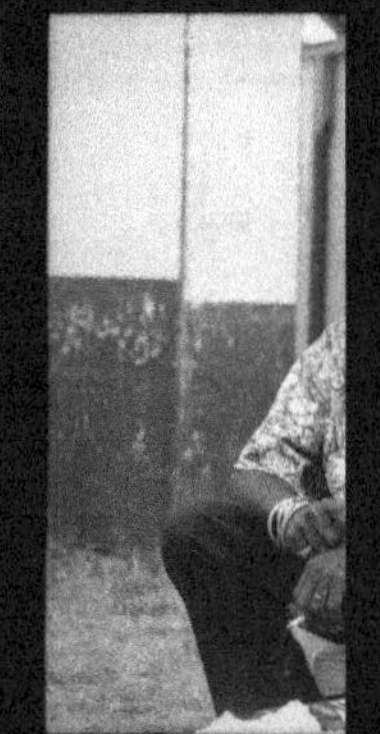

→20   →20A   1 8 1   →21A

FILM 5060   KODAK SAFETY FILM 5060   KODAK

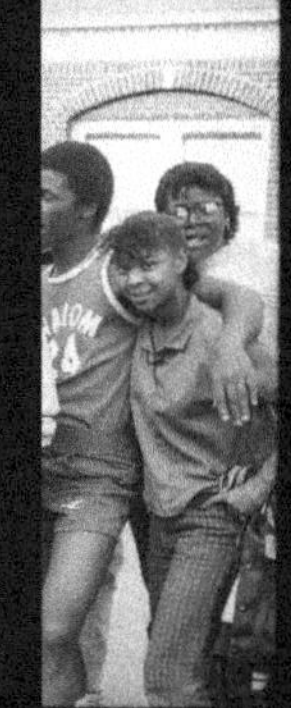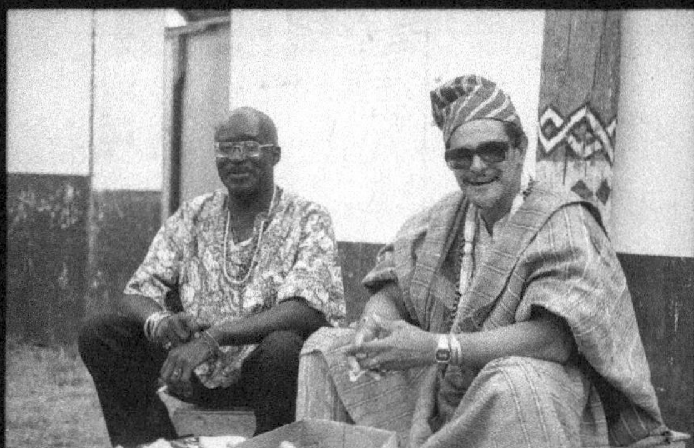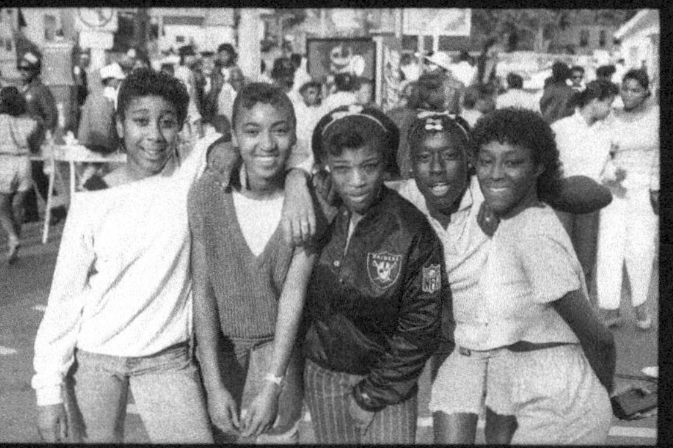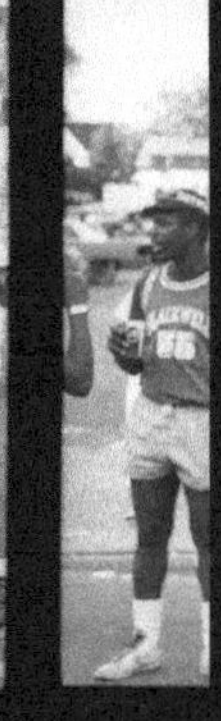

→21A   →22   →22A   →23   →23A

KODAK SAFETY FILM 5060   KODAK SAFETY FILM 50

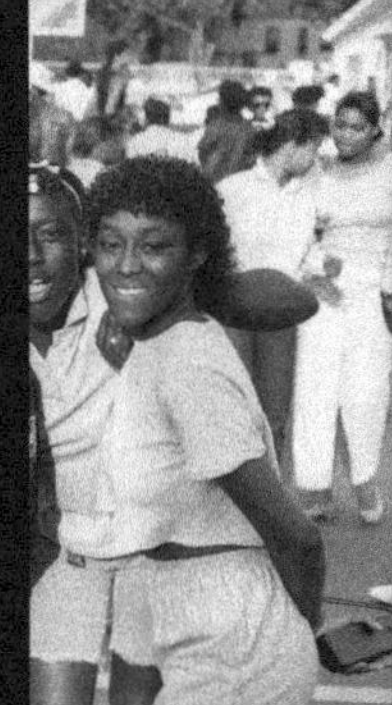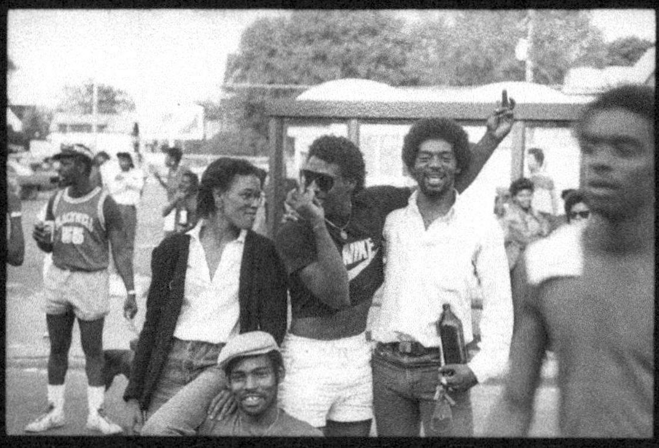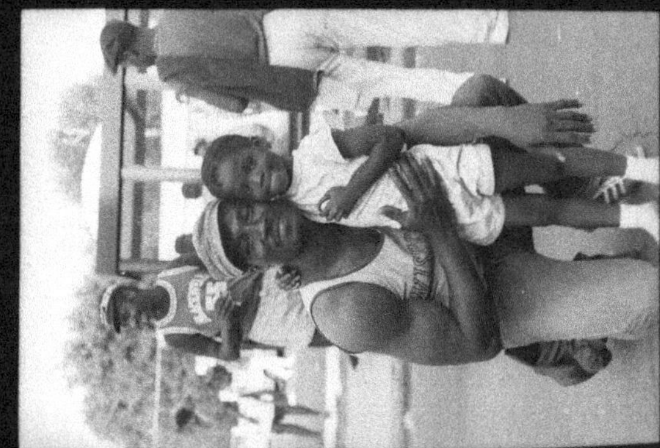

→23A   →24   →24A   →25   →25A

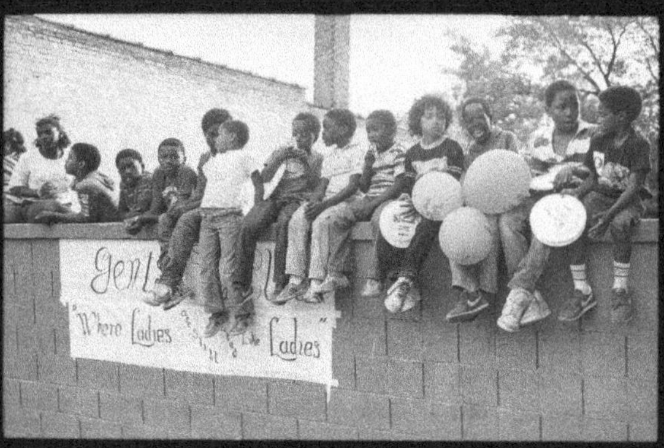
Gent
"Where Ladies Like Ladies"

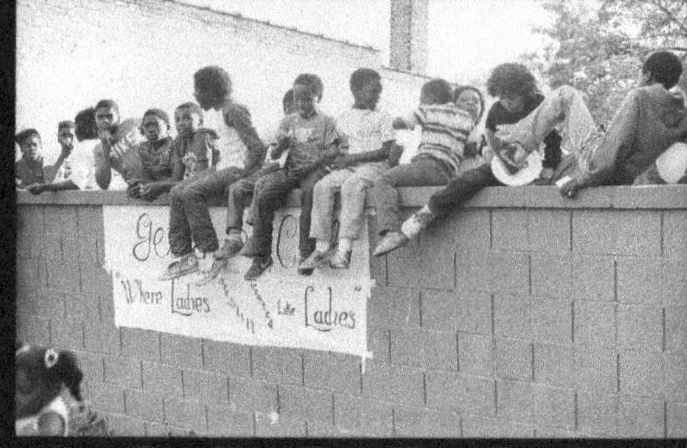
Ge
"Where Ladies Like Ladies"

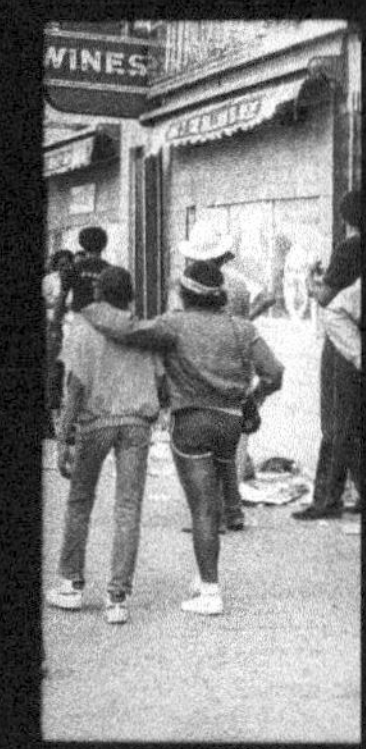
WINES

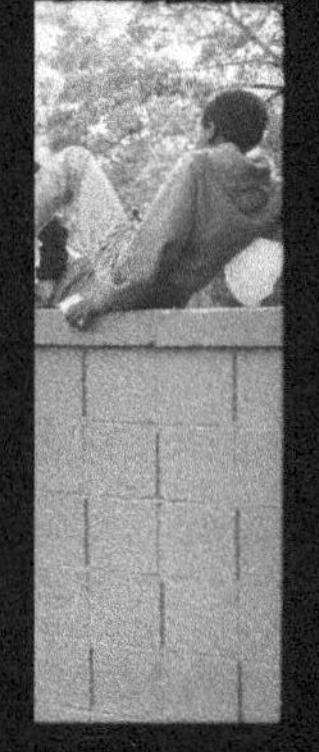

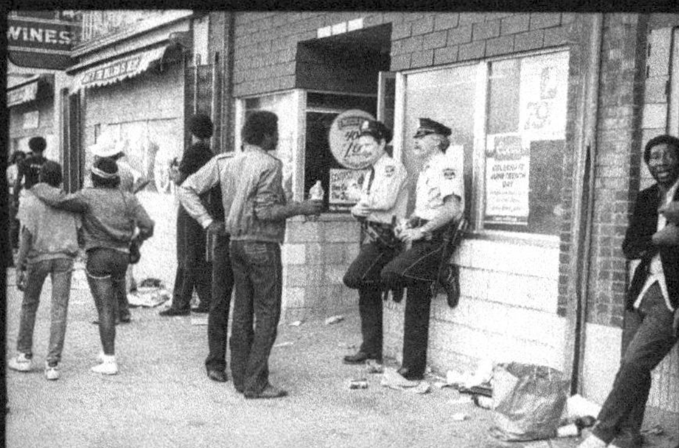
WINES

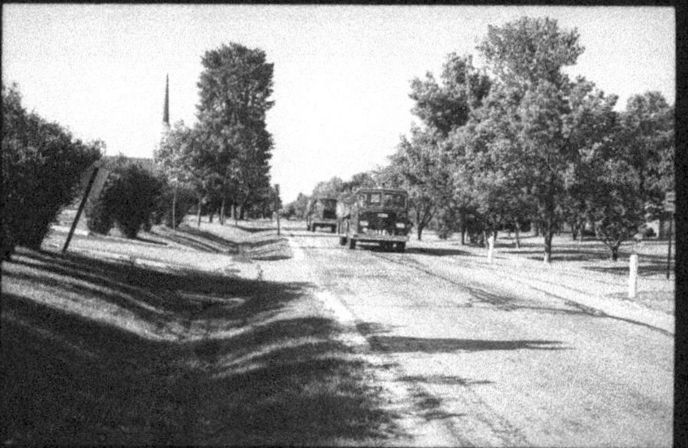

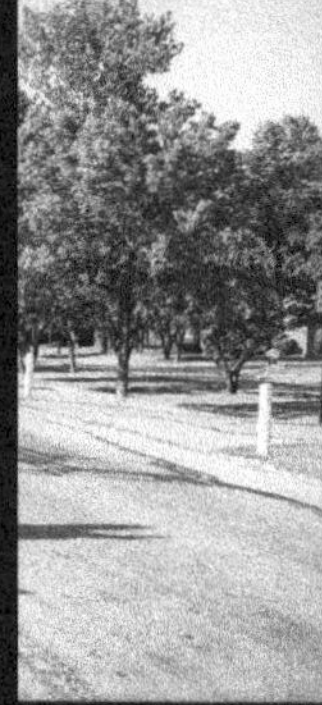

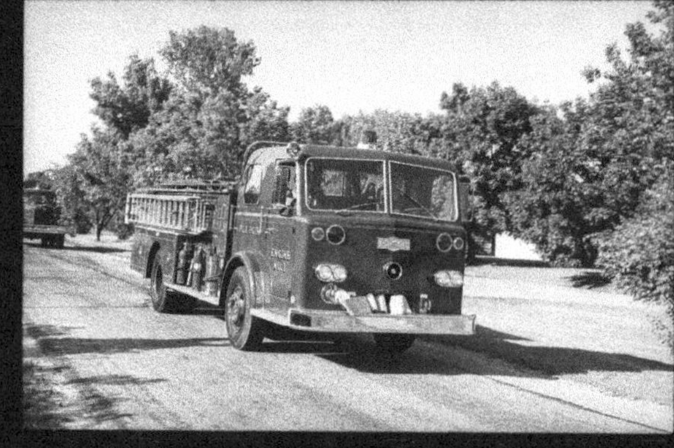

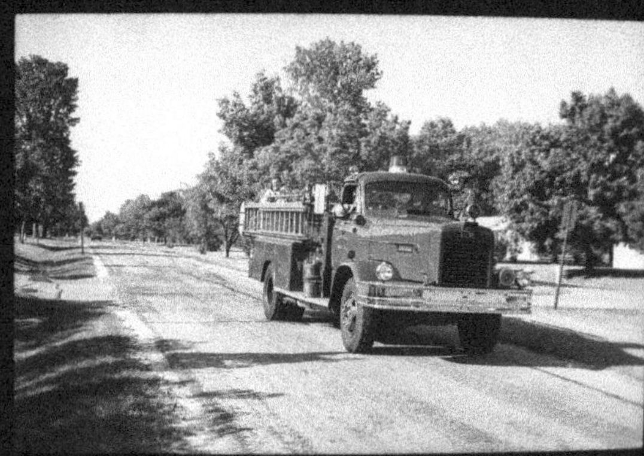

KODAK SAFETY FILM 5060
KODAK SAFETY FILM 5060

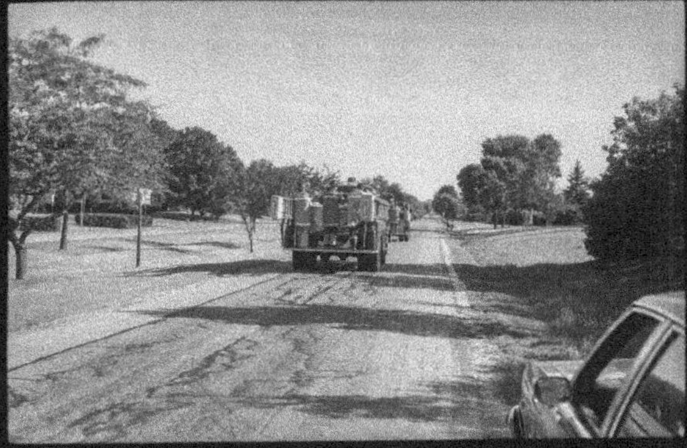
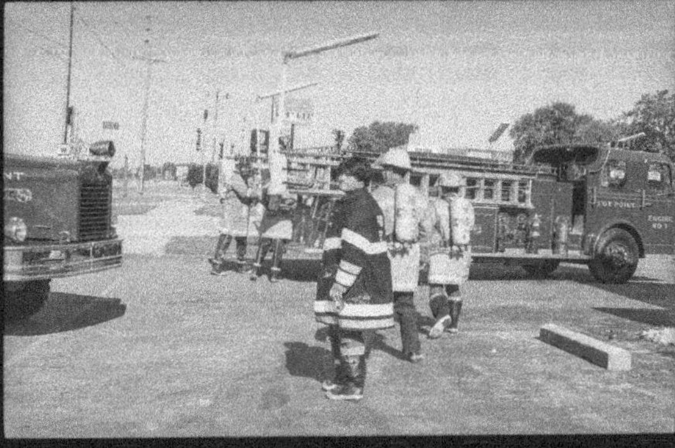
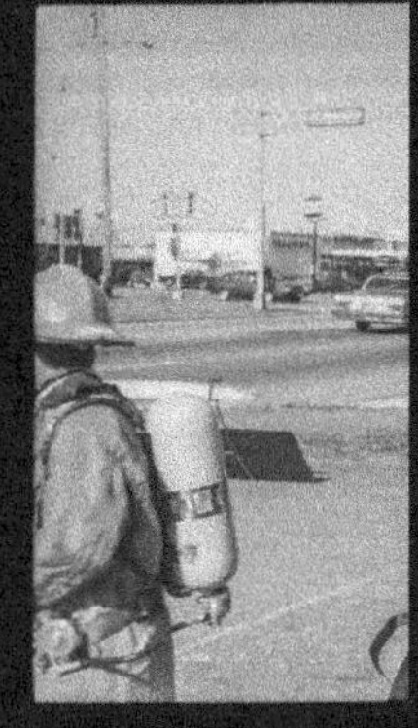

→ 32   → 32A   → 33   → 33A   → 3

TY FILM 5060   KODAK SAFETY FILM 5060   KOD

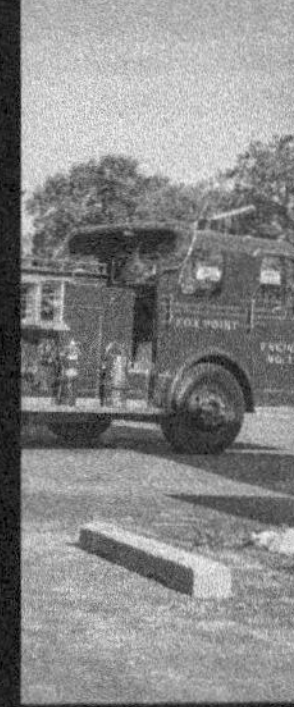
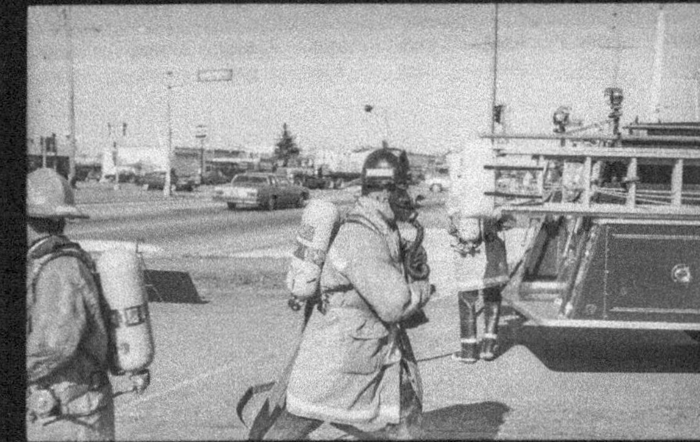
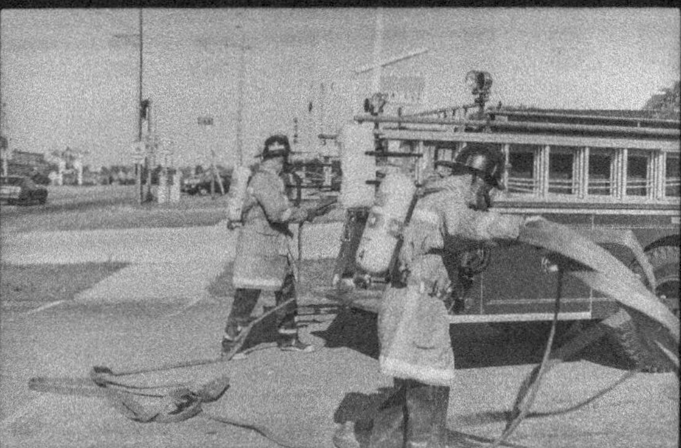

→ 33A   → 34   → 34A   → 35   → 35A

KODAK SAFETY FILM 5060

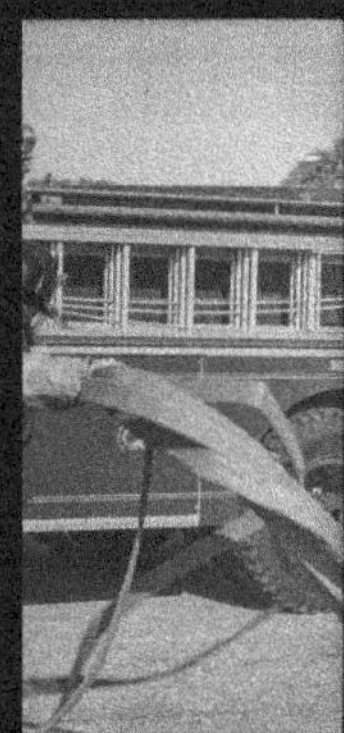
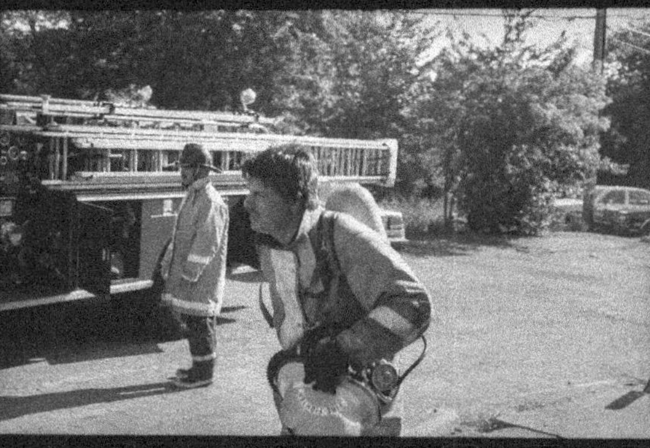
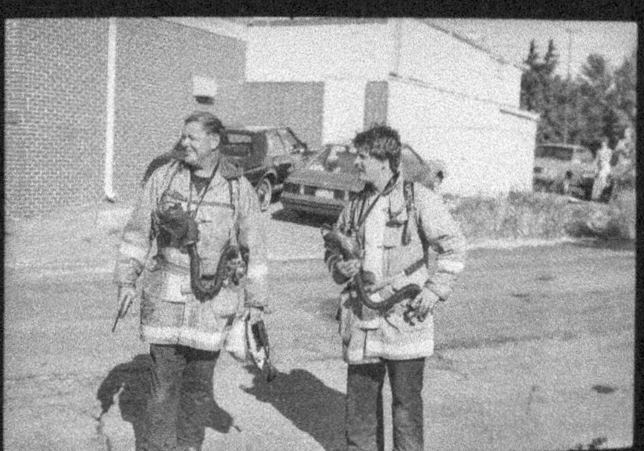

→ 35A   → 36   → 36A

Also from Anarchy Acres:

Rosie's New Harness
Popcorn Day
Haystack Rumors
A Dream for Anabelle
Kitchen Chaos

www.anarchyacres.com